AF553704

Creativity in Student Teachers

CREATIVITY IN STUDENT TEACHERS

By

Dr. T. Rajasekhar Reddy

DISCOVERY PUBLISHING HOUSE PVT. LTD.

NEW DELHI-110 002

First Published-2004
Reprinted-2011

ISBN: 81-7141-770-1

Published by:

DISCOVERY PUBLISHING HOUSE PVT. LTD.
4831/24, Ansari Road, Prahlad Street
Darya Ganj, New Delhi-110002 (India)
Phone: 23279245, 43764432 • Fax: 91-11-23253475
E-mail: discoverypublishinghouse@gmail.com
parul.wasan@gmail.com
info@discoverypublishinggroup.com
Website: www.discoverypublishinggroup.com

Printed at:
Mehra Offset Press
Delhi

Foreword

It gives me great pleasure in writing foreword to the book entitled "Creativity in Student Teachers".

Teaching in general, emphasizes on drill and grill in the acquisition of new data and information and in their utilisation. It is not wrong if we say that education system is reducing the originality and creativity of the teacher and the taught. Any novel classroom situations occur only accidentally and not by any design.

It is now realised that any system of education in a society should encourage creativity so that a society can be saved from stagnation and the individual also can have his own fulfilment. It is heartening to note that creativity has entered in to the curriculum of the schools. Research studies are now conducted on the nature of creativity nurturing of creativity, instruction that can help the development of creativity measurement and prediction of creativity and so on. Keeping in view the importance of the teacher in developing the creative thinking among learners, the present research work was conducted by the author.

The main objectives of the study were to study: (1) the level of creativity among student teachers of DIETs, (2) the influence of personal, social, psychological variables on creativity and (3) to predict creativity with the help of selected bunch of independent variables. Creative thinking was judged on the basis of the verbal and non verbal creativity scores obtained on all the components of creativity-fluency, flexibility and originality.

The salient features of the study are: The investigator has developed clear conceptual frame work based on the statement of the problem. The literature scanning is comprehensive and adequate. An adequate and representative sample was drawn.

The methodology adopted for data collection, presentation and discussion is excellent. The statistical work is solid. The step wise regression analysis was adopted to predict creativity with the help of all the personal, demographic and psychological variables as predictors. The research work is presented in a logical, cogent and lucid manner. Thus the thesis maintains high standard of excellence.

The creativity of lectures is no less important than that of students. The present study is limited to the assessment of creativity the student-teachers of the DIETs. An attempt may be made by any research scholar to study the creativity of the lecturers and its effect on the creativity of the student teachers of DIETs. It is only creative teacher that can fruitfully implement creative programmes in the DIETs.

With the explosion in knowledge, no education can acquire or impart all the information pertaining to a subject. The best that one can do is to make the students cultivate a taste for reading. For cultivating the habit of reading, good books with in the reach of students are essential. I am sure that this book disseminates useful information to the students about the creativity and student-teachers of the DIETs.

I hope the DIETs, B.Ed. Colleges, M.Ed Departments of Education and State Departments of Education will make the best use of this book. Further, I hope that advanced students, teachers and research scholars interested in teacher education will find this publication of great value and interest.

Prof. N. Venkataiah
Principal
Institute of Advanced Studies in Education
Sri Padmavathi Mahila Viswavidyalayam
Tirupati-517 502, A.P.

Preface

The greatest joy of the teacher and the greatest hope for better world lies in the cultivation of creative power. Creativity is the main source of emergence and development of human culture. A creative person is the product of a number of abilities and favourable personality traits. Each field of creative work requires certain basic abilities creative products are novel constructs. This novelty is a result of this interaction with the materials of his environment in divergent ways.

Primary education occupies the most important place in the ladder of education. The teacher training Institutes of Primary level which are now called as District Institutes of Education and Training (DIETs) play an important role in producing quality teachers for primary schools. Are these institutions producing creative teachers? Then who is an effective teacher? What are the qualities or characteristics of a good teacher? What criteria should be followed in the selection of candidates for teacher training and which type of educational programme should be given for them? A variety of such questions are to be answered with empirical evidence.

The research study was conducted in 1999-2000 to collect data about the creativity of student teachers of DIETs in Rayalaseema Region of A.P. employing the tools, Achievement Motivation, Scientific attitude and 16 personality factors of student teachers of DIETs. I am grateful to Dr. N. Venkataiah, Principal Institute of Advanced Studies in Education, Sri Padmavathi Mahila Viswavidyalayam, Tirupati, for writing a valuable foreword to the publication.

I express my sense of gratitude to Professor S. Padmanabhaiah Director, State Resource Centre Hyderabad for having given me an opportunity to work under his able guidance and also for his continued interest and encouragement for the publication of this book.

My grateful thanks are due to all those who have helped me for completing the study and in publishing the book.

T. Rajasekhar Reddy

Acknowledgement

I am proud enough to express my profound respect, deepest admiration and sincere thanks to my research supervisor *Prof. S. Padmanabhaiah,* M.A. M.Ed. Ph.D., for his valuable guidance and constant help throughout the research study. His critical comments, enlightening discussions and innovative ideas have been instrumental in the successful execution of the investigation. I am very much indebted to him for the suggestive encouragement provided for the successful completion of the thesis.

I sincerely wish to tender my heartful gratitude to *Dr. P.S. Geethanath,* Senior Lecturer, DIET, Karvetnagar, Chittoor District for his constant encouragement and good wishes also for his invaluable guidance in selecting the problem and unaccountable interest and untiring help all through the work, which has enabled me in the successful completion of the research work.

I should render my sincere, thanks to *Dr. B. Ramachandra Reddy,* Principal IASE, Head of the Department of Education, for his many valuable suggestions in connection with the investigation. I am also indebted to *Dr. D. Ramakrishanaiah,* Associate Professor, Department of Education and *Dr. V. Dayakar Reddy,* Associate Professor, Department of Education for their help whenever I approached them during the tenure of this study.

I wish to express my thanks to principals of DIETs for their cooperation and students who participated in providing the required data for the investigation.

I am very grateful to my family members and my friends for their constant help and cooperation. I express my thanks to my wife Mrs. B. Aruna M.A., M.Ed., for her kind help at various stages of the investigation.

T. Rajasekhar Reddy

//

Contents

1

Introduction

EDUCATION FOR EVERYTHING

Education has been recognized as a fundamental right and it is viewed as a process of human resource development where the knowledge, skills and capabilities are sharpened to achieve a wide range of objectives. In a democracy, education can be used for giving training in good citizenship. It can produce leaders in different walks of life. Under democracy, education produces individuals capable of independent thought, judgement, self expression, originality and initiative.

Education is the process by which an individual is enable to function according to the expectations of the society as well as according to his/her capabilities. Locke (1969) stated 'plants are, developed by cultivation and men by education'. According to Pestolozi 'it is the natural, harmonious and progressive development of man's innate powers'. Rousseau recognises education as a process of development. It is the natural development of humanity, the spontaneous development of all our innate nature and faculties.

Article 45 of our constitution upholds the states right and duty to provide free and compulsory education for all children until they complete the age of 14 years. Again Article 29, 30 and 41 speak of the citizens right to education and culture.

The aim of education is to develop an integrated personality, suitably stuffed and equipped from all dimensions. viz, physical, mental, moral, emotional and vocational. Education does not mean imparting of verbal knowledge. The knowledge that is gathered in schools should be capable of being used for all the life situations, service to society and helping to improve the deplorable conditions of ones own country. The Characteristics of true education are humility apart from developing intelligence and skills and power of discrimination.

It is now realized that any system of education in a society should encourage creativity so that a society can be saved from stagnation and the individual can also have his own fulfilment. Thus, we find that creativity is entering into the curriculum of a school as well as in its evaluation. Studies are being made about the nature of creativity, how it grows, how it can be nurtured, what instruction can help its development, how it can be measured and predicated, and so on.

QUALITATIVE IMPROVEMENT OF EDUCATION

Education in our country does no good in any qualitative aspect. Teaching emphasizes on drill and grill in the acquisition of new data and in their utilization. According to Bloom (1958) there is some reason to believe that education system can reduce originality and creativity. This negative effect on creativity is mostly marked when examinations, instructional materials and processes, all emphasise learning by rote and the goal is centered on getting through and examinations. Any novel class room situations occurs only accidentally and not by any design. Though the topic creativity was recently introduced in the teachers training courses, most of the teachers are ignorant of the concept of creativity.

The new education policy stresses equalization of educational opportunities, recognition of education at different stages with special emphasis on quality improvement, efficiency and effectiveness at all levels, reorienting the content and process of education, utilization of modern communication technologies, an over bowling of the system of planning and management of education. In view of these imperatives the policy regards education as a crucial area of investment for national development and survival.

The National Policy on Education (1986) States: 'The new thrust in elementary education will emphasize two aspects, (1) Universal enrolment and Universal retention of children up to 14 years of age; and (2) a substantial improvement in the quality of education'. Regarding the process of learning, it further states 'child-centered and activity-based process of learning should be adopted at the primary stage'. During the past decades considerable efforts have been made and are being continued to implement and National Policy on Education, particularly with regard to elementary education and teacher education.

To achieve Universal enrolment and Universal retention of children up to 14 years of age, primary schools have been established with in easy reach of all children and teachers and people of the community are involved in Universal enrolment and retention. At least two teachers have been provided in every primary school and school education facilities have been improved through, 'Operation Black Board' (OBB). Community has been involved in primary education through establishment of school education committees. House to House surveys are made to locate unenrolled children and parents are persuaded to send them to school.

The Second main focus in elementary education by the National Policy on Education is "Considerable improvement in quality of education", (I) improving school, facilities through Operation Black Board and (ii) Improving the quality of the teacher through pre-service and in-service education of the teacher programme of Mass Orientation of School Teachers (PMOST-1987) for effective implementation of UEE. Through the 'Operation Black Board' Scheme, primary schools all over India were provided with considerable educational equipment by the Government of India. The National Council of Educational Research and Training (NCERT) and the State Council of Educational Research and Training (SCERT) State Institutes of Education (SIEs) in collaboration with Regional Institutes of Education (RIEs) have also organized massive in service education programme for primary teachers. For qualitative improvement of primary education, the syllabus of primary classes in each subject has been re-organised in terms of minimum levels of learning (MLL) and teachers have been oriented in teaching strategies for enabling pupils to achieve mastery levels in the MLL. To improve teacher Education at the elementary level, District Institutes of Education and Training

(DIETS) were established at the district level which were provided with adequate well qualified staff and better educational provisions for pre-service teacher education of good quality as well as to organise in-service education for primary teachers of the district.

Imbibing the spirit of the policy provisions, the District Primary Education Programme (DPEP) emerged in 1994 as a response to various challenges in the primary education sector. The programme seeks to 'Universalise' primary education by revitalising the existing system. It seeks to identify and tackle 'inefficiencies' by integrating innovative practices and approaches. Adopting 'area specific approach' with district as the unit of planning, the key strategies of the programme have been to retain the contextuality and sensitivity to local conditions and ensuring full participation of the community. There is a marked focus on sustainability, equality and local ownership.

NEED FOR A CREATIVE TEACHER

Any improvement in education whether quantitative or qualitative can be secured only through the efforts of teachers who are the direct agents in the process of education. Children with good character, right tastes, sound knowledge, and worthy capacities are essentially the products of able teachers. The education commission has rightly said that 'the future of India is now being shaped in her class rooms'.

The teachers, therefore, are the most potent factors for preparing children not only to fit in to the democratic, secular and socialistic pattern of the country but also to meet the various challenges posed in life.

Hence, it is very important to plan for the preparation of the teachers in such a way according to such standards that they are properly equipped to plough this important role. The teacher is no longer a subject teacher only. By implication he is a practical psychologist, a hygienist, a guidance expert and what not. It is needless to emphasise, therefore, that the teacher does not perform a single function called 'teaching', rather he is in turn a lecturer, counsellor, educator, questioner, encourager, coach, listener, arbitrator, friend, critic, interpreter, helper and judge among others.

The importance of the teachers in the educational programme of a country is too great. The greatness of a country does not depend on lofty building, gigantic projects and large armies but on the quality of its citizens. If a nation has youngmen of sterling character and unimpeachable patriotism, she is found to make rapid progress in all fields. Youngmen are entrusted to the care of the teacher and it is therefore the sacred duty of the teacher is to impart the right type of knowledge and make them good citizens. It is the teacher who impresses his children with his personality.

The teacher, a national integrator as he is, the backbone of society, particularly so in the remote villages. He stands as an outstanding figure among the illiterate and semi-illiterate families. The teacher actively shares there responsibility of reconstructing a social order, with all the cherished values and traditional beliefs which are being eroded by the surge of new ideals and practices.

"No system of education, no syllabus, no methodology, no text book can rise above the level of its teachers. If a country wants to have quality education it must have quality teachers".

V.S.Mathews

"Of all the different factors which influence the quality of education and its contribution to national development, the quality, competence and character of teachers are undoubtedly the most significant.

Indian Education Commission, 1966 (p.46)

WHAT IS CREATIVITY?

Thus, there is no substitute to a quality teacher. A quality teacher is effective in realising the goals of education. If he is creative many more innovative learning activities will be created by him to make the success rate of learners at the peak.

Creativity is the main source of emergence and development of human culture. The present day scientific and technological progress has been made possible through creativity. Music, Painting, Poetry, and other forms of art that give us not only pleasure and joy, but also lend a new meaning to life, are all products of creativity. Let us imagine thousands of years back, in some primitive habitation, there was a man, endowed with a spark of creativity, who for the first time thought of planting a seed, or who devised a wheel, or who decorated the walls of his rock shelter with drawings of animals. These were the persons, who not satisfied with the pattern of life and ways of carrying out day-to-day activities, boldly thought of something new. They were followed by countless others whose creative endeavours have leld to the comforts, facilities, and enriched life that we enjoy today.

Creativity is too complex in nature. Different view points have been put forward to explain the concept emphasising different aspects of creativity. By and large, psychologists seem to agree that creativity involves the ability to produce original ideas and to perceive new relationships among unrelated things. However, creativity is multifaceted.

Recently creativity has been identified with genius a divine gift and people of exceptional calibre are considered to be possessing such supernatural abilities. This view is attacked by modern psychologists and they totally rejected this conception. They agree that it is an ability of mind, like intelligence and is possessed by all individuals.

Imagination is considered as synonymous with creativity. Andrews (1930) defines imagination in children as the process by which items of experience are combined to form new products. Griffiths (1945) differentiated imagination, a mode of thinking concerned with fantasy and day dreams from imagery, a type of sensory experience in which images arise independent of external stimulation. The term creative imagination has been used by MCcloy (1939) O'Brien, Sibley and Ligon (1953) and Greenacre (1959) where as McDowell and Howe (1941) refer to productive imagination. All these investigators considered newness or originality as the main criterion. The term 'imagination' is more often used to describe the process rather than the product.

The word creativity has its origin in an Indo-European word 'Kere' which means 'to create something'. Hence, it means 'to create something novel'. Novelty implies originality, uniqueness and uncommonness. In brief creativity refers to originality of some utility. Guilford (1962) defined originality as the production of unusual, farfetched, remote or clever responses, presented in terms of the statistical infrequency of response among members of a certain population that is culturally homogeneous.

In general, four approaches have been used to understand the concept of creativity. These are called the four Ps, that is, the product of creative thinking (product), the process of creative thinking (Process), the person who is creative (person) and the press or the environment in which the creation comes about (press).

A creative person is the product of a number of abilities and favourable personality traits. Each field of creative work requires certain basic abilities. In the absence of requisite abilities, creative work of a high order can hardly be expected. But abilities in themselves are not enough. A person may be highly gifted so far as the abilities are concerned but may be lacking in drive and task commitment. Such a person can hardly be expected to make any notable contribution. Besides drive and task commitment there are other personality traits that prepare the necessary ground for creativity to blossom.

The credit for initiating systematic research in creativity goes to Joy Paul Guilford (1897-1987). Guilford was elected as the President of American Psychological Association in 1950 and the title of his presidential address was 'creativity'. The address has been taken as a milestone in the study of creativity. Guilford's major contribution to creativity is his concept of divergent thinking as given in the structure of intellect model. According to him there are two types of thinking divergent and convergent. Later in place of thinking he substituted the word 'production' because he considered these two types of thinking as productive operations.

From the point of education, the most important point is that children can be creative or at least they can experience the process of creativity. This experience will help in developing in them a creative attitude. The creative attitude is a kind of belief that human ingenuity can find a solution to almost all problems, which can be more or less satisfactory, that improvement is possible in all things, institutions, and organisations that poverty and suffering can be reduced and life can be made happier, that the dimensions of knowledge have no limits and a search can be rewarded with new discoveries.

Creativity is uniqueness. It is thinking in divergent directions. Creativity suggests utmost freedom of human thought.. The creative individual is free to choose any path that is open to him. It is viewed as involving the production of as many answers as possible to a given problems. In a particular situation, creative individ[illegible] may behave in his own way which is different from that of his fellow beings and thus leaves the stamp of his own creativity is sharply differentiated from stereotyped behaviour. Creative products are novel constructs. This novelty is a result of his interaction with the materials of his environment in divergent ways. The uniqueness, novelty or originality or creativity is evident form the creative works by artists, musicians, scientists, painters, and the like.

CORRELATES OF CREATIVITY

The increasing awareness about the importance of creativity is generating many more research questions. What factors promote creativity? How far do these factors contribute towards the development of creativity? There are non-organismic variables like demographic factors and sociocultural factors. The variables in the second category are organismic variables, such as intelligence, achievement and personality factors.

Studies having non-organismic correlates of creativity considered variables like age, birth order, sex etc., and correlates of achievement are categorised under the heading of demographic correlates. The other variables like locality, socio economic status etc., have been categorised under sociological correlates of creativity.

A number of studies have been carried out on the relationship between creativity and different variables but by and large the obtained results were not equivocal.

Sex and Creativity: Contradictory trends of results could be observed on the relation between creativity and sex who are more creative boys or girls? Results of research are not equivocal on this aspect. Three contradictory trends of results are observable on this issue (i) Males are superior to females in creative thinking (ii) Females are superior to males in creative thinking (iii) There are no sex differences in creative thinking ability.

Age and Creativity: Raina M.K. (1970) studied the relationship between the variables of age and total creativity and its components. Of these, the variables of total creativity, originality and elaboration were found to be positively and significantly related with age. Lalithamma M.S. (1973) observed that creativity and age were positively and significantly related to each other. Khire U.S. (1971) and Badrinath. S and Satyanarayan, S.B. (1979) reported that creativity increases up to the age of 13 years, whereas, Joshi R.J., (1974) and Ghakar, S. (1974) found that creativity increases up to the age of 15 years. Mc cloy (1939) showed that imaginative behaviour correlated more highly with mental age than with chronological age. Torrance (1962a) examined changes in performance on creativity tests and found the following generalised pattern in increase in creative thinking abilities from ages. During the age 12 to 14 years the individual tends to respond to adventure more rapidly than to reason.

Locality and Creativity: In 1969 a study was conducted by Aaron, Marihar and Malatesh in which they explored the differences in creativity among rural and urban students. Singh, Joshi and Chandrakant also found that there was no significant difference in the creativity of urban and rural students.

Creativity and Birth Order: What is the relationship between birth order and creativity? Unfortunately there appears to be little consensus as to what this relationship is most of the research in the area is indirectly focused on family influences and child rearing practices. Srivatsava. B. (1978) Jarial, G.S. (1981), Dave, J.G., (1981), Sharma H.L. (1986), Raina, K. (1986) and Santhana, K.S. (1990) found that first borns were superior to laterborns with respect to different components of verbal creativity on the otherhand Srivatsava, S.S. (1977), Srivatsava, R. (1978) Badrinath. S.and Satyanarayana, S.B. (1979) and Sharma, K. (1982) reported no significant difference in the veral creativity of students of different birth orders. There is a need to examine these findings with respect to the nature of the in-home environment elements like, child rearing practices, size of the family, Joint nuclear family and liberal conventional outlook. The nature of sibling relations, the feeling of being isolated during childhood. Over-protectiveness by Parents, recognition of autonomy and non-conformity and broken homes, might be influencing the creative growth of children. Eisenman and Schussel have concluded that later born males are significantly less creative than the first born males on the three measures of creativity.

Personality and Creativity: A few researchers have studied creativity in relation to personality traits. They also tried to discover the role played by these personality traits in specific creative activities. Research questions have been possed asking whether creative individuals exhibit high sensitivity, aesthetic sense, initiative and performance for perceptual novelty?

The relationship between creativity on one side and locality, annual income, birth order, family literacy index, parent's occupation on the other also did not yield stable results.

From an analysis of the different studies carried out on creativity it may be observed that most of the studies were conducted on primary or secondary school children. Further not many studies have come to print on the differential effect of achievement motivation, scientific attitude and personality factors on the creativity is taken in this study.

DEVELOPMENT OF CREATIVITY

Some studies that have been conducted show that creativity develops with age and experience. Several other investigators have found it to be otherwise. By implication, one can hopefully infer that if conducive environment and methods are deliberately provided, creativity can be developed.

There are a large number of methods for developing creative thinking. Such as: brain storming, brain calming, mind control, synectics, morphological analysis, bionics, random stimulation, value engineering, free association, scenario writing, altered states of consciousness, awareness development, bio feedback training, deep relaxation, creative dreaming, gestalt therapy, enhancing incubation, socio drama, psychodrama, meditation, sensitivity training, sounds and images, analogies, attribute listing and scamper, reversal method, destructuring—restructuring etc., some of these have been tried out by different researchers in the field of education. A great amount of research was conducted on the psychological nature and measurement of creativity during the decade of 1960's comparatively less emphasis was laid on development of creativity.

According Guilford (1967) creative problem solving may be an important key to the solution of many of humanity's most pressing social problems. If this is true, training in creative problem solving will be greatly needed and research on creativity training is a necessary prerequisite to the design of instructional programme.

According to Maltzman, *et al* (1959) training in the production of responses increased the originality of verbal association and that the results tentatively support the hypothesis that originality is a form of learned behaviour following the same principles as other forms of operant learning. Meadow and Parnes (1959) found that the group receiving instruction through the experimental programme attained significant increments on the measures of quantity of ideas as well as quality of ideas. The creative problem solving course produced a significant increase on certain ability measures associated with practical creativity as well as the personality variable-dominance.

Nirpharake (1977) attempted to develop and test an integrated programme of training in creativity for high I.Q., low creativity children. For the purpose of training four vital areas of creativity, namely perception, divergent production, evaluation and appreciation and problem solving were selected.

The sample consisted of 36 boys in grade VII in Poona city with superior intelligence and normal level of creativity. The training programme consisted of 100 sessions. 25 sessions to each area of creativity. The procedure followed includes introduction and instruction, short lecture followed by discussion, demonstration, exercises and again followed by discussion, procedures like group problem solving and role playing were also utilised. The study showed fruitful results at the end of the training. The performance of the experimental group was better than that of the control group on creativity tests given after training.

Vandana (1979) applied discovery method for teaching physics to high school pupils in which the theory course was integrated with laboratory work. The experimental group was taught the unit 'light' in physics by discovery method and students were given full freedom to play with the apparatus on the other hand the control group was taught the same unit by the tradition method. The findings showed superior performance of the experimental group over the control group both in achievement and creativity tests. The to values were highly significant at 0.01 level indicating effectiveness of the discovery method over traditional method.

Vora (1985) prepared a programme known as a divergent thinking programme in marks. 3 matched groups were selected for experiment of which 2 were experimental and the third was control group. The programme contained three types of problems multiple response, hidden shape and make up problems. The programme was organised for six weeks. The results showed that the experimental groups were significantly superior in their creativity compared to the control group.

Shively and Feldhusan (1972) attempted to asses the differential effectiveness of two creativity instructional programmes which support to develop similar skills and abilities among pupils of same age, as well as the influence of the teacher on the effectiveness of the instructional programme. The two instructional programmes, the productive thinking programme and the purdure creativity training programme (Feldhusan, Bhalke and Treffenger 1969 speedie and Trefflenger 1971, Robinson 1969) were used under active or restricted teacher participation which will be labelled 'discussion' and 'non discussion' respectively. Sixteen fifth grade teachers and 317 pupils in the public schools in Northern India participated in the study.

Both programmes produced significant gains in many of the conditions of use. But over all for all criteria, the productive thinking was more effective than the purdue creative thinking programme.

The means for verbal fluency and flexibility were higher for children whose teachers were higher in creative ability and used the productive thinking programme with no discussion. Hence, the teachers creativity level might influence the effectiveness of the programme, ideally the teachers creative level should be high.

Malhotra and Rita (1985) took two groups of ten students each, matched by paired comparison method in a senior model school. Experimental groups were given brian storming treatment in 20 sessions of 25 minutes each as per the rules and procedures laid by Osborn. The finding revealed a significant difference between experimental and control groups in favour of the experimental group, after the training.

Bhooder Singh (1987), Khatena (1973) found that factors of general creativity can be influenced by a specially designed teaching strategy. According to Davis (1973) and Torrance (1972) creative thinking abilities of children can be enhanced by many diverse means.

Tracy and Rand (1979) made an attempt to enhance student's creative thinking on an individualised self paced basis. The research vehicle used for the study was the purdue creativity training programme (P.C.T.P.). It is a set of programmed materials that has been the focus of several previous investigations. It consists of 28 audio taped stories. Presentations of each was accompanied by a printed exercise for the development of verbal and figural creative thinking abilities.

The study involved utilization of the P.C.T.P. on a self instructional basis. Research with the P.C.T.P., and other programmed creativity instructional materials led to an expectation that the programme would be effective on a self instructional basis. In this programme the teachers role was deliberately held to a minimum. Teacher gave the instructions, played the tapes and distributed the exercise sheets. The results indicated that several programmes, including the P.C.T.P., were successful in enhancing creativity with minimum teacher interaction.

Reese, Treffinger, Parnes and Sounis (1976) studied the effect of a four semester creative studies programme upon a broad range of measures from Guilfords (1967) structure of intellect. In this project, however, creativity was defined as including several cognitive operation.

In an experiment of Trainable Mentally Retarded (T.M.R.) children conducted to determine the effect of training in attention and concentration and open ended activities in promoting creative thinking skills in T.M.R children, it was found that there was a significant improvement in the experimental group with regard to the verbal creative thinking ability.

According to Thomas (1981) there was a significant development of creativity in the children who got instruction from the teachers who were trained in formulating questions requiring congnitive memory, convergent thinking and evaluate thinking responses.

Burstiner (1973) designed a study to investigate the effects of a workshop in creative thinking and problem solving for Departmental chairman of public secondary schools. Ss were seventy four chairman from various school districts on Lon Island and from the New York City. The experimental group (48 subjects) participated in an extensive 8 week workshop programme in creative thinking and problem solving that had been specifically designed for school department heads.

There were three phases in the workshop activities. 1. Introduction to creative thinking. 2. Training in creative problem solving techniques and 3. Practice in group and individual problem solving. Supplemental reading of Osborn's (1957) 'Applied imagination' was required. The activities embraced to a considerable extent much of the material outlined in the instructors manual (Parnes, 1966) of Creative Education Foundation.

Analysis of co-variance yielded significant differences (P<.01) on six of the seven sets of scores. In appraising the findings, it must be concluded that the effects of participation in the workshop were largely positive. The participants scored significantly higher in the total quantity of ideas generated and in the adjudged originality and usefulness of those ideas.

It would appear that training in creativity thinking and problem solving skills could enable the high school department chairman to improve their capabilities, with in the supervisory aspects of their position. Similar workshops should be considered for teachers, administrators and non certified personnel, a step towards the solution of school problems and towards smooth integration and functioning of such personnel components with the school.

Pillay G.S. (1977) employed multifactor covariance design having experimental and control groups to find out the effect of 'creativity teaching method' upon the general creative thinking of eighth graders and their achievement in geography through creativity teaching method i.e., combination of Brain storming and morphological analysis. The investigator gave 33 lessons on units of teaching from geography of which fifteen were through creative teaching methods. The results indicated that the creative teaching method produced no differential effect upon general creative thinking, its sub-parts or on creative thinking in geography. But experimental group produced higher mean performance scores on achievement in geography whereas the traditional method produced higher mean scores in memory.

CREATIVITY AMONG STUDENT TEACHERS OF DIETs

Primary Education occupies the most important place in the ladder of education. The progress and achievement in the higher stages of education depends upon the effectiveness of the primary education. Further, it is a stage where the desirable skills, attitudes and thinking pattern are to be developed in a germinal manner failing which, much unlearning and relearning is to take place in the later stages. Primary education should in its natural status, be such as to attract and retain children throughout the primary stage and create an urge for further education or self study.

Every child who comes to this world has some inclination of mind, intelligence and tendency. He is usually active and has attachment with worldly objects. The child has tendencies of good and bad. The child begins to learn from the very beginning of his life and develop his tendencies. Through education and teaching, he is able to remove his bad or beastly tendencies and grow in to a human being or a social animal. If he does not amend his beastly tendencies it may be difficult for him to make himself a true human being.

The process of successful learning of knowledge, skills and attitudes, where what is learned is worth while in the learner and usually where it is learned in such a way that the learner can express his own individuality through what he learns and can subsequently apply it, and adopt it flexibly, to situation and problems other than those he considered in learning it. Also, education is used to refer to the product of the above process, and to the academic discipline studying the nature of the process and its outcomes.

Education is complex affair and rich in its implications. However, it may be said that education enables the pupils to acquire the required knowledge and awareness to have useful insight into the world at large. It is a valuable tool of transforming the out dated, unhealthy and ineffective tendencies of men into dynamic, healthy and vigorous development of the personality as a whole. As educationists feel what is required now a days is man-making education. The recent trends and reforms in the field of education are directed towards the realization of such main objective.

The primary stage of education covers roughly the children of age 6+ to 12+ studying class I to VII. This is a very crucial stage in the life of the child. The child's spontaneity, curiosity, creativity and activity in general should not be restricted by a rigid and unattractive method of teaching and environment for learning.

THE PROBLEM

Creativity is more than a word today. It is an incantation. It is a kind of psychic wonder creative talent makes history through reshaping man's world. The progress of any civilization depends upon new insights, fresh ideas and original productions. The future of a nation that does not recognise this fact, to say the least, will be at peril.

Creativity is an asset to any nation, which needs creative scientists, engineers, technocrats, economists, poets, painters musicians etc., development and progress in different areas of national life depends on creative children. Creativity is not restricted to the choosen few. All children are creative and its dimensions vary from child to child.

The concept of creativity is as old as the Hindu vedic literature, but widening interest in creativity in the last few decades has lead investigators to examine more closely the beginnings of creativity in children. According to Butcher (1972) "Any society to avoid stagnation, needs a constant supply of original ideas at all levels, but profoundly original men who are the most fertile source of these ideas are often the very people who most disturb the society by threatening its established ways of thought and familiar structure". Yet they are needed, nay, they are most needed to assure betterment of mankind.

Today the focus of the entire world is on this specialised area "Creativity". Research in the field of creativity has been an outcome of this realization. The present interest in the creative or inventive process through which the mind produces new and useful ideas arises from a growing realization of the importance of new ideas for the success of an individual or a nation.

In recent years it has frequently been proposed that there is a separate aspect of intellectual functioning not sampled by conventional intelligence tests. Guilford (1959) has suggested that this is because conventional tests are heavily saturated with convergent thinking" skills and take little account of "divergent thinking".

According to Arasteh and Arasteh (1976) research on creativity and the development of talent have proceeded from both childhood and adulthood with an obvious gap in the adolescent period. In this view of creativity Torrance (1964) has commented of the divergent educational levels, the primary school years have been the most neglected in creativity research.

There are several aspects of creativity on which clear answers are yet to be found out by sustained empirical research. In today's highly technological society the critical demand for inventive scientists and engineers has highlighted the need for some means of identifying those individuals with the greatest creative promise. In education where creative qualities have been neglected in both testing and teaching it is desirable to assess each individual's creative potential in order to determine what he needs to develop that potential. Hence the study aims at finding student teachers creative potentialities. How does creativity develop during the adolescense? What are the effects of variables like, Achievement motivation, Scientific attitude, 16 personality factors and personal and social variables on creativity? — are some of the questions to which answers will be found with the empirical evidences.

Any research in the field of education should bring an increased understanding of the existing phenomenon and lead to further refinement or improvement in the educational practices if it is an applied research and it should add to the existing stock of knowledge if it is a fundamental research.

The present study virtually analyses the existing pattern of student teacher training at DIETs at primary level and so it falls under the category of applied research.

In this connection it is worthy to mention the saying of an eminent educationist— "As is our education, so as is our nation, as are our teachers, so is our education but as is our teacher educational programmes and selection of teacher-trainees, so are our teachers". The emphasis here is on the selection of teacher trainees and giving them a suitable teacher educational programme. It is obvious that these two are the determining factors of our nation's future. That is why 'the destiny of our nation is being shaped in her classroom'.

Society wants good and effective teachers to teach younger generations. Then who is an effective teacher? What are the qualities or characteristics of a good teacher? In order to produce effective teachers, what criteria should be followed in the selection of candidates for teacher training, and which type of educational programme should be given for them?

The greatest joy of the teacher and the greatest hope for better world lies in the cultivation of creative power. "To teach toward creativity is to teach toward the future of society' (Lowen field and Britain, 1966).

What is necessary is to bring about the optimum development of the whole individual. To realise this aim, we have to teach the child to think creatively about the yet to be discovered" (Crutchfield,1967).

RESUME OF THE SUCCEEDING CHAPTERS

Chapter II deals with a brief review of research work done in this field. Chapter III gives an account of the statement of the problem with its objectives and a little description of the variables that are considered in this investigation and the different hypotheses to be tested.

Chapter IV gives an account of methods employed in the investigation, such as development of the data gathering instruments, selection of the sample collection of data, scoring and analysis.

Chapter V deals with the results and discussion, it includes 1. Description of the distribution 2. Influence of personal and demographic variables on creativity 3. Influence of Achievement motivation and scientific attitude on creativity. 4. Influence of personality factors on creativity. 5. Prediction of verbal, non-verbal and composite creativity.

Chapter VI deals with summary of the investigation and major conclusions arrived at. It also gives the educational implications of the study and the suggestions for the further research.

2

Review of Related Literature

CREATIVITY—CONCEPTUALIZATION

The Almighty God is the creator of the Universe. He is the supreme mind who possesses the finest creative abilities. He has created all of us and all that is revealed in nature and nurture. According to our Indian Philosophy, we all are constituents of the supreme power as the rays of the sun are the constituents of their creator-sun. Therefore every one of us ought to possess creative abilities and it does happen. All of us possess these abilities. But as we find that every one of us is an unique creation, thereby the degree of possession of creative ability is not uniform. Some of us are found to possess high creative talents and these are the persons who move the world ahead by their discoveries and inventions in the field of art, literature, science, business, teaching and other fields of human accomplishments. They are responsible for putting up new ideas and bringing about social and cultural changes.

Creativity is as old as human history. It is the creativity on the part of man that distinguishes human beings from other animals. The history of human progress and development in a variety of directions in the history of human creativity itself. Creativity may be regarded as the highest faculty of man, the greatest talent of human being, which is basic to all his achievements. Human creativity gets delineated into different spheres of his behaviour. In the fact creativity was considered synonymous with intelligence, in sight and intuition. A good deal of confusion in this area arises from loose usage of terms like creative, original imaginative, non conformist, non conventional, gifted, talented, genies etc.

A few thousands of years ago man was barbaric and brutal. He was just like an animal staying in caves and eating the raw flesh of animals. When the first ray of creativity flashed into his mind no one knows because every new way of life, every deviation from the set pattern is an evidence of creativity. His inner self would have started thundering due to his innate creative potentialities like an ocean surging with its roaring waves, ever since he started thinking to adjust himself to the environment.

The history of man's creativity is fascinating. The deeper we plunge in to the ocean of creativity, the more we unearth and the richer we become in terms of the progress of civilization and the comforts of life. There was an era of the bullock cart and no more than that was known, when the pedestrian probably envied the comfort the traveller in the bullock cart enjoyed. Then came the era of the steam engine. John Stevenson started with a dream—a dream of running, faster and he created crude and clumsy engine with a speed of just a few miles an hour and now his engines are running at 200 kms per hour. Wright brothers imagined flying like a bird and they created an ordinary aeroplane and now it is replaced by jet planes.

Creativity is man's greatest asset. It is the most highly valued qualities of human being. There is no gainsaying that it is a source of emergence, development and survival of man's culture. The functioning of the mind and the nature of human genius is the centre of mental ability has become the focus of research activity only when Guilford propagated has theory of human intellect. His theory gave a good base for research in the area of creativity.

Though the concept of creativity is as old as the Hindu vedic literature, it has entered into the researchers parlance only recently. Guilford in his presidential address of the American Psychological Association in 1950 become spark that kindled scientific research on creativity. Guilford statement only summarises the elusiveness of creativity for systematic research.

Systematic educational research in creativity is as new as it is a fruitful field of endeavour. The problems are as complies, the concepts are as uncertain, and the results often as conflicting as the subject is enticing and vital, whether it is about the relation between creativity and intelligence about the threshold hypothesis or about the possibility of fascinating creativity in the class room, there seems to be almost as many points of view as there are studies.

It is needless to mention that schools put more emphasis on cognitive achievement than on creativity. Some school practices such as rigid scheduling may even hamper creativity. Guilford stated that the bulk of research on creativity has left little doubt as to which of the two personal orientations convergent or divergent, receives greater attention in most of our educational institutions.

Education has emphasized abilities in the area of convergent thinking and evaluation after at the expense of development in the area of divergent thinking. We have attempted to teach students how to arrive at correct answers that our civilization has taught us are correct. This is convergent thinking outside the arts, we have generally discouraged the development of divergent thinking abilities unintentionally but effectively (Guilford, 1957).

In every sphere of knowledge such as medicine and surgery, technology and electronics, agriculture and industry, transport and communication, philosophy, psychology and literature there is vast development which is only through creative genious of man.

Creativity may be thought of as quality or talent leading to a result which is novel and useful. The process involves interplay among a person a task and a social environment. Creativity springs from inner most recesses of human vision. It is found in all human beings.

Scientists like Einstein, Newton, Edison, Darwin, Galileo and Bhaba entered into the materialistic world and unravelled thousands of mysteries where as Kalidasa, Valmiki, Keats and Shakespeare entered into the humanities voyaged beyond the known. Christ, Buddha, Kabir, took their own voyage and realised their real self. All these creators have enriched the world with their creativity.

The world is changing rapidly. The change is bewilderingly fast. It may not be an exaggeration to say that the discoveries of the next twenty years may make the last 100 years to have progressed at snails space. We may not be able to foresee today what type of knowledge one needs five or ten years hence, to meet his life needs. We will indeed, need different kind of thinking process, for different from the conventional thinking that we are accustomed to, to be able to live in a world which is changing so fast.

The new perspective of understanding human creative potentials had been the demand of the age as the then existing knowledge of intellectual abilities was insufficient to explain the psychological bearings in creation, because of the psychological bearings in creation, because of the complex nature of intellectual or thinking abilities involved in creation, on the one hand and the increased scientific, industrial, technological, educational, artistic, pursuits that essentially need them on the other.

In the second decade of the last century when experimental psychology was on its way, the concept of creativity captured the attention of the association with this school of thought. For example Mill (1843) asserted that very many ideas can be knit together by association in to complex idea and that the nature of the complex resultant is to be understood by the fact that all the components are still actually present in it.

The concept of creativity was first recognised by Galton (1869) with his publication of 'Men of Genius'. Galton did not seriously attempt to understand the mental operations by which distinguished leaders produced their novel ideas, but rather he tried to understand the hereditary nature of creative performance. He demonstrated that creative individuals came largely from families in which their relatives have also been creative.

In dictionary of Education creativity is defined as the quality thought to be compassed of broad continua upon which all members of the population may be placed in different degrees. The factors of creativity are tentatively described as associative and ideational, fluency, originality, adaptive and spontaneous flexibility and ability to make logical evaluations.

Creativity concept is notoriously difficult to in down because it had been used synonymously with terms like "Imagination", "Ingenuity", "Spontaneity" productivity, originality, divergent thinking, inventiveness' intuition, 'venture sameness', exploration' and 'giftedness' child (1973) observed that there is no clear, unambiguous and widely accepted definition of creativity. What child has said in 1973 is probably equally true even to day.

Galton (1869) in his publication of 'Men of Genius' recognised creativity as 'trait'. Andrews (1930) defined imagination in children as the process of which items of experience are combined to form new products. Griffiths (1945) differentiated imagination, a mode of thinking of concerned with fantasy and day dreams, from imagery, a type of sensory experience in which images arise independent of external stimulation. The term creative imagination has been used by Mccoly (1939) Greenacre (1959) and O'Brein, Sibley and Ligon (1953) where as McDowell and Howe (1947) refer to "productive imagination". All these investigators considered newness or originality as the main criterion.

Imagination and 'fantasy' have been interchangeably used. Both Griffiths (1945) and Singer (1961) equate fantasy with day dreams and imaginative play and the resulting images thereby produced. The term imagination' is more often used to describe the process rather than the product. Singer differentiated early fantasy, characterized by verbal role taking, from later internalised fantasy, chiefly of a visual type.

Generally consider as an important component of creativity, originality is defined in terms of relative infrequency of a response within a particular group. Guilford (1962) defined originality as the 'production of unusual', farfetched, remote or clever responses presented in terms of the statistical infrequency of a response among members of a certain population that is culturally homogeneous". Torrance (1962) accepts Guilford's definition with the added proviso that the response is relevant to the task, shows intellectual strength or represents some breakaway from the obvious the common place and the banal.

Doppett (1964) defined creativity in terms of achievements labeled as creative by 'judges'. To study the judgemental process the author devised a series of 'test' items describing various behaviours which the respondent rates for creativity. All items depict only fictitious events, scientists, artists and business people will be asked to rate these descriptions and they themselves will be evaluated in an effort to find answers to such questions as (1) what kind of behaviour are considered creative by acceptable judges? (2) Do judges qualified in different areas rate creativity in similar or different ways? (3) which of the emotions associated with the achievement seem to be related to the creativity ratings? (4) what factors in the backgrounds of the judges are related to ratings made by them.

Whether, creativity is to be defined and studied in terms of 'process' or 'product', constitutes a major issue in much research. This issue has been dealt with by Gallangher (1963), Golamn (1961) Jackson and Messick (1965) Stein (1962) and Taylor (1964). Studies of creativity in children have primarily concentrated on the process of creative development.

In general four approaches have been used to understand the concept of creativity. These are called the four Ps, that is the product of creative thinking (product), the process of creative thinking (process), the person who is creative (person) and the press or the environment in which the creation comes about (press).

(i) Product Definitions

According to the Dictionary of psychology creative thinking means 'the achievement of new relationship among the parts of experience, which according to Walls (1926) has four stages, Preparation, Incubation, Inspiration or Illumination and Verification. The creative idea comes as a flash of insight or a sudden thought (Harriman, 1947). Hutchinson (1949) says 'by creative effort I mean the initiation and execution of some work of literature, art, music or science which is essentially new'.

Creativity as a combination of many abilities running through many spheres of human activity. It is manifested in a variety of ways though essentially it is the process of bringing something new into birth "(May, 1953). The creative thinker is one who explores new areas and makes new observations, new predictions and new inferences. (Gray, 1954).

Creativity is the capacity of a person to produce compositions, products or ideas which are essentially new or novel and previously unknown to the producer (Isrelle and Drevdahl, 1956). According to Morgan (1960) creativity involves development of something unique by the individual. Don Mackinnon (1962) the criterion for creativity is a statistically infrequent response or idea that is adaptive and sustained to fruition, 'mere novelty of a product does not however, justify its being called creative... the product must be adaptive to reality.

An omnibus identification has presented by Newell and others (1962), which states that thinking may be called creative if (1) the product has novelty and value either for the thinker or the culture, (2) the thinking is unconventional, (3) it is highly motivated and persistent or of great intensity, and (4) the problem was initially vague and undefined so that part of the task was to formulate the problem itself. The above statement has the advantage of inclusiveness but, like other omnibus conceptions it has the disadvantage of being an inventory without a unifying rationale.

Rogers (1962) and Arnold (1962) insist on a tangible product such as a poem, a work of art or scientific theory as an indicator or scientific theory as an indicator or creativity.

Gatzels (1964) has attempted to deal with creativity along somewhat different lines, giving primacy to nature of the problem rather than to the solution. A distinction is made between presented and discovered problem situations, the former involving a problem that is already formulated, the later a problem that stills needs formulation. The significant element in creative performance according to Gatzels and Csickezentimihalyi (1964) is the envisagement of the relative problem for it is the fruitful question to which the novel solution is the response.

Parner (1966) defines creative behaviour as that 'which demonstrates both uniqueness and value in its product'. According to Barron (1969) creativity may be defined quite simply, as 'the ability to bring something new into existence'.

Guilford (1971) expresses that creativity is an ambiguous word, but when it is used in the phrase 'testing for creativity', its meaning may be restricted to those qualities or traits of individuals that predispose them to produce novel ideas and novel effects.

According to Wilson, Guilford and christianson (1974) creative act is that in which "something new is produced—an idea or an object including a new form or arrangement of old elements". The new creation must contribute to the solution of some problem.

Creativity in education as the 'emergence of new concepts' and views it as the end product of spatiotemporal process (De Roc-Adrian, 1974). Three conditions are required (a) originality of response, (b) adaptability and (c) elaboration.

Jha (1978) defined creativity as 'the manifestation of uncommon talent in terms of novèl and original products' (whether ideas or effects) commanding high professional estimate of their worth.

(ii) Process Definitions

The starting point in creative process is a felt need which initiates the effort. Not every one experiences this need. One can just be happy and contented, as many are in carrying out the routine. The two aspects of creativity, the process of creation and the product of creation—there is no definite opinion as far as the former is concerned because it is almost an inner happening and it differs from individual to individual.

Simpson (1922) defines creativity as the..."..... initiative which one manifests by his power to break away from the usual sequence of thought in to an altogether different pattern of thought".

Patrick (1935) studied the creative process in fifty known artists and fifty non-artists who were equated for sex, age, race and fluency. The investigator suggests that in the process of creativity four stages emerge: preparation, incubation, illumination and verification or revision though there may be some overlapping.

Osborn (1948) the father of Brain-storming and a pioneer of creative education, divides the creative process in to the following phases.

Orientation (Picking out the problem)

Preparation (gathering relevant material the organization effort). Analysis and ideation (seeking possible solution).

Incubation (a time lag for the mind to synthesise the problem and solution).

Evaluation (Putting the pieces together and verifying the solutions through further testing or evaluation).

We should not be deceived by the seeming simplicity of this procedure. It is simple enough to be effective but it certainly is not automatic. In fact the creation of new ideas will require tremendous mental effort. Perhaps that is why it is after said that creativity is 'painful' Thomas A. Edison once commented that creativity is 90 per cent perspiration and 10 per cent inspiration.

Freud (1948) holds that "sublimation of repressed unconscious wishes and pregenital and libidinal urges determine creativity".

According to Ghiselin (1952) creativity is a process of change and development in the psychic life of an individual leading to invention.

Fromm (1959) defines the conditions of creativity as the capacity for wonder, the capacity to face incongruity and tension, to orient oneself towards the new, to be aware of experience and to respond fully, to such awareness.

Creativity is an activity which brings something 'new' and which has utility. Thus creativity reshapes the horizons of human understanding (Staine, 1960)

According to Mason (1960) creativeness in the best sense of the word, requires two things on original concept or idea and a benefit to some one.

Golann (1961) creativity is a normally distributed trait, an intra psychic process and a style of life. Mednik (1962) defines creative thinking as the process of forming associative elements in to new combinations which either meet specified requirements or are in some way useful.

Hallman (1963) has analysed the creative act into five major components.

1. It is a whole act a unitary instance of behaviour.
2. It terminates in the production of objects or of forms of living which are distinctive.
3. It evolves out of certain mental processes.
4. It co-varies with specific personality transformation; and
5. It occurs with in a particular kind of environment.

Arnold (1963) says, creativity involves the rearrangements of past experiences with possibly some changes in to new patterns to satisfy some experienced or implied need.

Mednick (1964) says that creative thinking consists of forming new combination of associative elements which combinations either meet specified requirements or are in some way useful. The more mutually remote the elements of the new combination, the more creative is the process or solution. Guilford (1964) has introduced 'the concept of psychological products' psychological products are those which occur mentally, sometimes without finding expression.

Ray Chaudhuri (1965) indicated that "the more sophisticated view has located in creativeness, originality, novelty, communication of emotional authenticity, applicability, social acceptance and some sort of combinatorial activity (Bruner, 1962, Hammer, 1961, Stein and Heinze, 1960) support this view.

Torrance (1965) "The process of creativity consists of sensing problems or gaps in information, forming ideas or hypotheses, testing and modifying these hypotheses and communicating the results. Sensing gaps sets into motion the process of creativity where in the individual strives to fill the gap and supply the missing elements.

Wallach and Kogan (1965) suggest a basically similar notion, greater creativity should be indicated by the ability to produce more associations and to produce more that are unique.

Maslow (1968) for one insists on the importance of the flash of insight transcendent sensation itself, without reference to whether it will ever result in anything tangible the salient issue is not 'inspired product but the inspired movement'.

Barron (1969) looks at creativity as 'energy being put to work in a constructive fashion. The creative act is free and independent force imminently inherent only in a person, a personality. Only something arising in original substance and possessing the power to increase power in the world can be true creativity. Creativity is an original act of personalities in the world". (Berdyeacv, 1969).

According to Passi (1972) creativity is a multi dimensional (verbal and non-verbal) attribute differentially distributed among people and includes chiefly the factors of seeing problems, fluency, flexibility, originality, intuitiveness and persistency.

Creativity means the ability to produce new forms in art or mechanics or to solve problems bynovel methods (Chaplin, 1982).

Goldenson (1984) creativity means the ability to apply original ideas to the solution of problems the development of theories techniques or devices, or the production of novel forms of art, literature, philosophy or science.

(iii) Experience Definitions

Creativity is an integrated harmony between the external world of reality and the individual's internalized needs (Vinake, 1952).

Maslow (1963) is a proponent of subjective experience in creativity. He emphasizes on the importance of the flash of insight the transcendent sensation itself without any reference to whether it will ever result in anything tangible. The important issue is not the inspired product but the 'inspired movement'.

The path of creative insight is often thin and dim. It is not a happening in which some abstraction bursts full blown in to consciousness, it is the result of intensive effort at seeking new structures of known information of a long mixing of ideas often 'felt' rather than cognized. It is only the jelling that we "know" Marrifield, (1976).

The Person

What sorts of people are creative? What are the abilities and qualities that seem to produce creativity? High creatives are usually differentiated from low creatives in terms of certain qualities. It is generally found that people are creative with in particular domains even though people who are creative in different domains may share common traits. Thus one may be a creative biologist but an uncreative novelist.

The Press

Another approach to understand the nature of creativity is in terms of the press. A potentially creative person may wither in an environment that does not foster creativity. The more congenial the environment for creativity, the more a person is likely to exhibit his creativity. What kind of environment hinders and facilitates creativity particularly at school, will be discussed subsequently.

MEASUREMENT OF CREATIVITY

"The attempt to measure aspects of creativity through tests have a long history," Taylor (1964). The factor analytical studies by Guilford inspired the great variety of so-called creativity tests not only in his terms but also in related principles as well.

Among the many tests the Mednick's Remote Association Test (Mednick and Mednick, 1964), built on associative theory, Flanagan's Ingenious solutions to problems Test (Flanagan, 1958) one of the few attempts at assessing creative thinking through multiple choice items, and the Ac test of creative Ability (Bhul, 1960), directed especially at problems of engineering. There are numerous other tests, including such other indices as the interpretation of Ink blots, block construction and drawing tests. Perhaps the most extensive set of materials for use at all educational levels is the Minnesota Tests of creative thinking (Getzels and Madaus, 1969).

Index of Creativity

The critical issue underlying all work in the field of creativity is the criterion problem according to Getzels and Csikszentmihalyi (1964). What is an appropriate index of creativity? Getzels and Madaus (1969) observed that the following are some among the most common criteria.

1. Achievement or Accomplishment

An attempt is made to identify achievements, which speak for themselves. At the adult level for example the Nobel Prize or some other mark of understanding accomplishment may be taken as an Index that hardly any one would dispute (eg., Ghiselin, 1952).

2. Ratings

It is assumed that a person who has an opportunity to observe another person can provide a sound judgement of his inventiveness. Evaluation by peers, supervisors and teachers has been used as a criterion (eg., Mackinnon, 1964, Drevdahl, 1964).

3. Intelligence

Performance on intelligence tests is the most widely used and best validated index of mental functioning. Presumably creativity is a mental function, and a superior IQ may be used as a criterion (eg., Termon, 1925).

4. Personality

Characteristics of personality are evaluated in relation to an empirically derived or on a prior profile of the 'Creative Personality' and the closeness of the fit is used a criterion (eg., Cattell and Drevalahl, 1955).

5. Creativity Test Scores

Performance on the creativity tests are such as those developed by Flanagan (1958), Bull (1960), Guilford and Merri. Field (1960), Mednick and Mednick (1964), Torrance (1964) and other. Chauhan and Tiwari (1974) surveyed the various Materials used for creativity testing and found that Inkblots, observations and drawings are some times used to assess creative ability of children. Poems, sketches, essays and stories written with the help of pictures are also used for the purpose, while creativity tests like word construction plot titles, unusual uses, consequences; mosaic tests etc., are frequently used to assess creativity amongst adolescents and adults by various researchers.

CREATIVITY TESTS DESIGNED BY DIFFERENT AUTHORS

1. Guilford Contribution

In 1958 when the Bureau of Educational Research of the

University of Minnesota began its studies of creative thinking, it felt that what was needed was a set of tasks which could be used from kindergarten through graduate school. Thus it first attempted to adopt Guilfords (1951) materials with this objective in mind.

The Bureau developed two alternate forms by following Guilford type of tasks. Unusual uses, impossibilities, consequences, problem situations, improvements, and problems. Adaptation was accomplished by substituting objects or situations more familiar to children. Thus subjects were instructed to think of unusual uses of 'tin cans' instead of 'bricks' and to imagine all the things that might happen 'if animals and birds could speak the language of men' instead of 'what would happen, if all national and local laws were suddenly abolished.

The Bureau's programme has been to develop complex tasks presumed to involve the creative process and then to examine the products for evidences of various types of thinking or to use Guilfords term, 'factors'. A calculated attempt has also been made to develop tasks which will grip the interest of the subject and which will permit him to 'regress in the service of the ego' which appears to be important in creative thinking (Schafer, 1958).

Three years of experimentation has resulted in the development and use of over twenty-five tasks varying greatly in the nature of the stimulus and the kind of thinking involved. All of them call for the production of divergent solutions, multiple possibilities, and some type of thinking involved, theoretically in creative behaviour.

Guilford has hypothesized that the thinking abilities involved in creativity were those he had defined as divergent productions and transformations. He included the redefinition abilities which were in the convergent production category of his structure of intellect and sensitivity of problems which fell in the evaluation category. Thus the following factors and tasks for assessing them may be regarded as summarising Guilford's present theory concerning the measurement of the thinking abilities involved in creativity (Guilford and Merrifield, 1960).

Factor	*Tests and Descriptions*
Sensitivity to problems (seeing defects, needs, deficiencies, seeing the odd the unusual, seeing What must be done)	Apparatus test: Suggest two improvements, for a common appliance Seeing problems—List problems that might arise in connection with common objects. Seeing deficiencies—point out the way in which a described plan or activity is faulty.
Figural spontaneous flexibility	Cube fluctuations-Indicate the number of changes in perspective of ambiguous cube (Thurstone) Windmill alterations—Indicate the number of alternations from one illusion to another while observing shadow of rotating rectangular blade (Thurstone). Retinal-rivalry reversals—Indicate the number of reversals when a blue field is presented stereoscopically to one eye and a yellow field to the other eye (Thurstone)
Figural adaptive flexibility	Match problems II. Indicate three or four different patterns of a specified number of matches that can be removed to leave a specified number of triangles or squares. Match problems III. Indicate several different patterns of matches that can be removed to leave a specified number of squares—planning air maneuvers—select the most direct path in 'sky writing' letter combinations (USAF).
Word fluency	Suffixes WI-Write words ending with a specified-suffix (ETS) Prefixes W_2-Write words beginning with a specified prefix (ETS) First and last letter W_3 write words beginning and ending with a specified letter (ETS)
Expressional fluency	Expressional fluency—write four word—sentences when the first letter of each word is given. Smile interpretations—complete a sentence that states an analogous idea. Word arrangements—write sentences containing four specified words.

(Contd...)

Ideational fluency	Topics if 1-write as many ideas as possible about a given topic (ETS) Theme if 2-write as many words as possible about given topics (ETS) Thing categories if 3-list the names of 'things that are round or that could be called round' Ideational fluency—write names of things fitting into broad classes.
Semantic spontaneous Flexibility	Brick uses (flexibility)-write a variety of uses for a brick Alternate uses—list different peculiar uses for common objects
Associational fluency	Controlled associations-write as many synonyms as possible for each given word Smile insertions—write objective completion for a smile. Associations IV-produce a word that can be associated with two given words Associational fluency I write synonyms for given words.
Originality	Plot titles (Clever)-write clever titles for story plots. Symbol production-produce symbols to represent activities and objects. Consequences (remote)-list, remote, consequences of certain changes.
Semantic elaboration	Planning elaboration—fill in as many details as necessary to make a briefly outlined activity work. Figure production—Add to given lines, to produce a meaningful figure. Score is based on number of details drawn.
Figural redefinition (defining or perceiving in a way different from the usual, established, or intended ways, use, etc.)	Concealed figures cf. 1-Indicate which of four complex geometrical figures contains a given geometrical figure (ETS) Penetration of camouflage—Locate faces hidden in pictures (USAF) Hidden pictures—Find human or animal picture hidden in a scene, as rapidly as possible (Thurstone) Hidden figures—Indicate which of five figures is hidden in a given figure.

(Contd...)

Symbolic redefinition	Camouflaged words—Find the name of the sport or game concealed in a sentence. Word transformation—Indicate new divisions between letters in new series of words forming a phrase, to make a new series of words
Semantic redefinition	Gestalt transformation—Indicate which of the five tested objects has a part that will serve a specified purpose. Object synthesis—Name an object that could be made by combining two specified objects. Picture gestalt-Indicate which object in a photograph will serve a specified purpose.

Getzels and Jackson (1962) constructed 5 tests to measure creativity. The tests are briefly described below:

1. **Word Association Test:** This test presents the subject with twenty-five words each of which has multiple meanings (eg. arm, cap, duck, fair, pitch, punch, sack, tender). The student is asked to write as many meanings as he can for each word.

2. **Uses Test:** This test presents the subject with the names of five common objects, (bricks, pencils, paper, toothpicks, paper clips, sheet of paper) and asks him to write as many different used as he can for each object. The idea for this test is derived from two similar tests used by Guilford in his factor analytic studies of cognitive ability.

3. **Hidden Shapes Test:** This test is part of Cattell's (1956) objective—Analytic Test Battery and consists of eighteen geometric figures each of which is followed by four more complex figures. The subjects task is to identify the complex figures in which the simple figure appears.

4. **Fables Test:** This test consists of four fables whose last lines are missing. The student is required to supply a moralistic, a humorous and a sad ending for each fable.

5. **Make up Problem Test:** This test consists of four complex paragraphs each containing many numerical statements, about activities such as buying a house,

building a swimming pool, and the like. For each paragraph the student is to use the information given to make up as many mathematical problems as he can within the time limit. But the problems must be capable of solution though he is not required to solve the problems.

Wallach and Kogan (1965) designed the following tests for measuring creativity.

1. **Instances Test:** It is the first of the verbal technique of the author. In this the child is asked to generate possible instances of a class that is specified in verbal terms.

2. **Alternate Uses Test:** It is the second of three verbal techniques. In it the child is to generate possible uses for verbally specified objects.

3. **Similarities Test:** In this the child is to generate possible similarities between pairs of verbally specified objects.

4. **Pattern Meanings Test:** This is one of the two creativity assessment techniques involving visual rather than verbal stimulus materials.

5. **Line Meaning Test:** In this second creativity procedure involving visual stimulus materials, the child is confronted with one or another kind of line drawings and is asked to generate meanings or interpretations relevant to the form of the line in question. The lines were adopted from Tagiuri (1960). Each line is a single continuous unit, in contrast to the discrete elements comprising the patterns in the proceeding instrument.

According to Arasteh and Arasteh (1976) the most systematic assessment of creativity is that made by Torrançe and his associates (1960a, 1960b, 1960c, 1961, 1962, 1962a, 1963a, 1964) who have administered the Minnesota Test of Creative Thinking (MTCT) to several thousand school children. These tests represent a fairly sharp departure from the factor type tests developed by Guilford and his associates, (Guilford, Merrifield and Cox, 1961;

Merrifield, Guilford and Gershon, 1963) and they differ too from the battery developed by Wallach and Kogan (1965) which contains, measures representing creative tendencies that are similar in nature (Torrance, 1968).

Torrance (1962) grouped the different subjects of the MTCT (Minnesota Tests of Creative Thinking) into three groups.

(a) Verbal tasks using verbal stimuli

(b) Verbal tasks using non-verbal stimuli and

(c) Non-verbal tasks.

A brief description of the different sub tests used by Torrance is given below:

Verbal Tasks Using Verbal Stimuli

1. **Just Suppose Test:** In the 'just suppose test' the subject is confronted with an improbable situation and asked to think of all the possible out comes from the introduction of a new or unknown variable. The verbal statement of the improbable situation is accompanied by a drawing of the situation. Blanks are provided under the verbal statement for responses. For example just suppose tongue one, get, caught in a big soap bubble and could not come out.

2. **Imaginative Stories Test:** The imaginative stories test calls for writing the most interesting and exciting story on a topic related to animals or people having same divergent characteristics. Topics such as the following are suggested 'The flying monkey'. 'The lion that won't Roar', etc. The child may use his own ideas and generate a new topic and write about it.

3. **Unusual Uses Task:** The unusual uses task calls for interesting and unusual uses of common objects such as tin, cans and book.

4. **Impossibilities Task:** The impossibilities task was used originally by Guilford and his associates (1951). But Torrance has made a number of modifications of the basic task. In this task the subjects are asked to list as many impossibilities as they can.

5. **Consequences Task:** The consequences task was also used originally by Guilford and his associates (1951). Torrance has made several modifications in adopting it. He chose three improbable situations and the children were required to list out their consequences.

6. **Situations Task:** The situations task was modelled after Guilfords (1951) test designed to assess the ability to see what needs to be done. Subjects were given three common problems and asked to think of as many solutions to these problems as they can. For example 'How would you handle a friend who likes to kid others, but cannot stand to be kidded by them'?

7. **Common Problems Task:** This was also an adaptation of one of the Guilford's (1951) test designed to assess the ability to see defects, needs and deficiencies. In this task the subjects were given common situations and were asked to think of as many problems as they can that might arise in connection with these situations. For example, getting to school easily in the morning.

8. **Mother Hubbard Problem:** This task was conceived as an adaptation of the situation task for oral administration in the primary grades. However it was found useful in older groups as a group administered task also.

9. **Improvement Task:** This was an adaptation of the Apparatus Test of Guilford (1952) which was designed to assess ability to see defects. In this task the subjects are given a list of common objects and are asked to suggest as many ways as they can to improve each object. They are asked to bother about whether or not it is possible to implement the changes thought of.

10. **Cow Jumping Problem:** The cow jumping problem is a companion task for the "Mother Hubbard Problem" and has been administered to the same groups, under the same conditions. The task is to think of all possible things which might have happened when the cow jumped over the moon.

Verbal Tasks Using Non-verbal Stimuli

1. **Ask and Guess Test:** It requires the individual first to think of all possible questions about what they see in a given picture, emphasis being on questions which can not be answered by just looking at the picture. Next he is asked to make guesses or formulate hypotheses about the possible causes of the event depicted and then their consequences both immediate and remote.

2. **Product Improvement Task:** In this task common toys are used and children are asked to think of as many improvements as they can which would make the toy more fun to play with.

3. **Unusual Uses Task:** Accompanied with the above (product improvement) task, another task (Unusual uses) is used. In this task the child is asked to think of the cleverest, most interesting and most unusual uses of the given toy other than as a play thing. These uses could be for the toy as it is or as it can be changed.

Non-verbal Tasks

1. **Circles and Squares Task:** In one form the subject is confronted with a page of forty two circles and asked to sketch objects or pictures which have circle as a major part. In the alternate form, squares are used instead of circles.

2. **Picture Construction or Shape Task:** In this task the children are given a piece of coloured paper of a given shape (a triangle or a jelly beam) and a sheet of white paper. The children are required to think of a picture in which the given shape is an integral part. They should paste wherever they want on the white sheet and add lines with pencil to make any novel picture. They have to think of a name for the picture and write it at the bottom.

3. **In Complete Figures Task:** This is an adaption of the 'Drawing Completion Test' developed by Kate Frank and used by Barron (1958). An ordinary white sheet is

divided into 6 parts (squares) each containing a different stimulus figure. The subjects are asked to sketch some novel object or design by adding as many as they can to the six figures.

Following similar procedure various tests have been developed by Mehdi (1973) Passi(1979) etc, to be used on Hindi speaking children.

RESEARCH ON CREATIVITY

While research on creativity is of recent origin even in the advanced countries, it is needless to point out that not many studies have been carried out in this area in the Indian context. A review committee was appointed by the Government of India in 1977 to review the whole curriculum and make suitable suggestions for necessary modifications. In its concluding remark the review committee emphasized the need for creative education.

If the purpose of education is to nurture the child capabilities to the full and to give our people not only a useful occupation but a full and abundant life, then the creative urge in the children must in every possible way be actively stimulated and cultivated in as many directions as possible.

One of the objectives of primary education, the NCERT has suggested, is that "the child should be able to express itself freely in creative activities and should acquire habits of self learning" (NCERT, 1975).

There are several aspects of creativity, on which clear answers are yet to be found out by sustained empirical research. For example, boys and girls differ in the various components of creativity like fluency, flexibility and originality, why does it so? How does creativity develop during the adolescent? and what are the effects of variables like achievement motivation, Scientific attitude and personality factors on creativity? These are some of the area of interest to researchers in the field of creativity.

Creativity and Personal and Demographic Variables

Creativity and Sex

The result of research on sex differences, especially in creativity are varied and hence are not conclusive. Who are more creative—boys or girls? Results of research are not unequivocal on this aspect. There are three contradictory trends of results are observable on this issue (I) Males are superior over females in creative thinking (ii) Females are superior over males in creative thinking (iii) There are no sex differences in creative ability.

There are several researchers reporting male superiority in creative thinking. Kelly (1965) for example observed that males scored higher than females on non-verbal creativity measures in his study on high school students.

Straus and Straus (1968) reported that boys performed better than girls on measures of creativity in both Indian and American Culture, while sex differences were more prominent in India. This finding was also supported by other Indian studies (Raina, 1968; 1969; Prakash, 1966 Gagneja 1972, Sharma, 1979, Dharmagandan 1981, Venkatrami Reddy and Balakrishna Reddy, 1984).

Awasthy (1979) found that male students were significantly higher than female students in fluency and originality areas. Boys scored significantly higher than girls in verbal originality and verbal total creativity Badrinath and Satyanarayana, (1979) Raina (1970) also observed that males were significantly superior to females in originality.

Torrance (1961) found that sex and age trends of creativity were evident even in the early grades. Torrance (1963) believes that from an early point in time girls are trained to accept things as they are.

On his tests of creative thinking, Torrance (1963a) found little difference in the ability of boys and girls until five years from then on boys begin to acquire superior ability in manipulating and experimenting whereas girls excel only in fluency of responses. Cultural sanctions apparently discourage girls from becoming interested in boys activities. However high school girls, who were given special training in science concepts subsequently demonstrated an increased ability to explain science principles.

The results contradict the common belief that boys are more creative than girls but also fail to support the hypothesis that girls would be more creative than boys. The higher creativity scores of the girls may be due to the fact that they come from a higher socio-economic class and thus were less restricted in expressing their ideas.

Rawat and Agarwal (1977) found that boys significantly counter performed girls in creativity. Dave (1980) and Shukla (1982) also found that boys were more creative than girls.

Mulkraj Tuli (1982) designed a study to explore the relation between Sex and Mathematical creativity. He found that boys were significantly more creative than girls.

Syama Thirumurthy (1987) also found that boys were significantly more creative than girls on a sample of 140 Gujarati speaking children (70 boys and 70 girls) were selected from four different schools. The interaction effect among the three independent variables sex, IQ and study habits was highly significant. It revealed that boys with high IQ and low study habits were, more creative than girls with low IQ and high study habits.

The second trend of observation that girls are better in creative thinking than boys is also supported by findings of quite a good number of investigations where children from first to sixth grade Wee involved Yamamoto (1960); MaC Gregor and Smith, (1965); Solmon, (1968) Walker, (1969); Cocha, (1971); Burgess, (1971) Torance and his associates found that in USA, after about the age of 10, girls consistently perform better than boys on almost every verbal test of creative thinking. Torrance (1967).

Chanda and Ghose (1985) found a statistically significant difference between males and females on all the components of creativity. The result is in line with those of Gatzels and Jackson (1962), Passi(1972), Hussain (1974) Singh (1975), Pandit (1976), Brodley (1976), Rawat and Garg (1977) Jurial (1981) and Chodha (1981) who found that females scored higher than males on all the four components of creativity.

Raina (1970) observed that females scored higher than males on all the dimensions of creativity except originality but these difference were not significant.

Bedi (1974) found a significant difference between the performance of males and females, in favour of females in measure of non-verbal creativity. Jayaswal (1977) found that female teacher trainees were significantly superior to male trainees on fluency and flexibility scores. Bharadwaj (1985) also found that verbal fluency was greater among females than males. Similarly Pandej (1984) studied the relationship better creativity and sex among high school students and reported that females scored significantly higher than males on elaboration.

Some investigations involving samples ranging from elementary school children through high school to college students however indicated no sex differences in creativity Phatak (1962), Pogue, (1964); Jackson (1968); Simpkins and Eiseman, (1968), Burns, (1969) Kaltsounis (1971), Phillips and Torrance, (1971), Kloss, (1972), Gakhar, (1974), Thamma Pratap, (1976), Dutt, Bountra and Sabharawal, (1977), Rasool, (1977), Check, (1979), Gupta, (1979) Saxena, (1981), Sharma (1981) and Jarial, (1981).

Olshin (1965) tried to determine what factors affected creativity and found no sex differences in creativity. Vohra (1975) also found no significant relation between non-verbal creativity and sex. Thorat (1977) conducted a study to compare the creativity of male and female student players and found no sex differences in their creativity scores.

From the findings on sex differences in creativity cited above one naturally gets the impression that the results are controversial, inconsistent and inconclusive, while concluding this section of review of literature we may cite one such controversial finding by two leading researchers in the field, viz Torrance and Harlow. Harlow (1967) reported that seventh and Nineth grade boys obtained higher scores on flexibility whereas girls obtained higher scores on originality on the other hand. Torrance in several investigations found that boys were more original than girls even though the girls scored higher than boys on most of the verbal measures of creativity.

Creativity and Age

Markey noted age changes in terms of frequency and complexity of imaginative responses as early as in 1935. He found that a child exhibited more imaginative play if he associated himself with older children than with those of his own age. Lehman found that highest quality production occurred most often in early thirties. The optimal years for chenists seem to be 26-30 years, for mathematicians 30-40 years, for musicians 30-40 years and philosophers between 35 and 39 years of age for writers specialised in specific field of literature, this Peak Period ranged between 27 and 45 years (Lehman and Heidler; 1949). Lehman has given some examples of exceptionally creative like Aristotle, Francis Bacon, William Crook, Leonord Euler, etc., whose contribution were outstanding even as teenagers. According to Rossman (1931) the most active period of productive thinking was 25 to 29 years.

In one of the foremost studies Mccloy (1939) showed that imaginative behaviour correlated more highly with mental age than with chronological age. Lehman's (1953) findings reveal that adult creativity matures early, reaches its highest point in the thirties and then gradually declines. These conclusions are, however disputed (Dennis, 1956).

Since, no systematic criteria of creative output can be established for children. Torrance (1962a) examined changes in performance on creativity tests and found the following generalized pattern increase in creative thinking abilities from ages 3 to 4½, a small drop upon entrance to kindergarten, a sharp decrement at about grade 4 and then, with variations by sex and certain sub tests, except for a small decrement at grade 7, a steady growth through grade II.

Simpson (1922) included grades three through eight in his studies of creative imagination. Starting with a low point at the beginning of the third grade, he found a sharp increase by the end of the year followed by a decline at the beginning of the fourth grade. This was followed by an upward trend until a peak was reached in the second half of the sixth grade, after which there was a decline in the seventh and a still further one by the beginning of the eighth. Mearns (1941) maintained that a decline which set in during sixth grade continued throughout the high school period. Unless revived by a special encouragement. He has drawn the above conclusion on the basis of experiences in stimulating creative writing but apparently without any measurement.

During the age 12 to 14 years, the individual tends to respond to adventure, more rapidly than to reason. In this period gifted children show remarkable performances in artistic, musical, mechanical and imaginative fields. The individual begins to question adult regulations and wants a share in decision making. He feels insecure however, because of changes in his physical and emotional makeup and a growing strangeness in interpersonal relation (Torrance, 1962).

For the individual between 14 and 16 much of the imaginative activity seems to be focussed on a future career. Adventure is still the key word for all Phases of life. The youth is able to see that there are no absolute solutions, to some problems, but he has not yet learnt how to apply creatively the principles he has learnt about right or wrong. According to Ligon, he can with practice make his emotions creative (Torrance, 1962).

Between 16 and 18 years the individual is able to think in terms of abstractions and to translate his social ideas into specific experiences. He can also channel his emotional energy in creative lines. During this period aesthetic interests and skills should be encouraged, 16 to 18 year olds need problems which require creative applications of what has been learnt. Adults should provide 'food for thought' for the adolescents during this age. At times the adults themselves may have to seek creative solutions when they find themselves in conflict with this age group of 16 to 18 years old (Torrance, 1962).

Raina (1970) investigated the relationship between age and total creativity along with its components and reported that total creativity, originality and elaboration were positively and significantly related to age.

Ahmed (1980) also reported a significant development in the verbal and non-verbal creativity from classes VII to XI Lalithamma (1973) also obtained similar results.

Khire (1970) and Badrinath and Satyanarayanan (1979) observed that creativity increased upto the age of 13 years. Joshi (1974) found that creating increased upto 15 years.

Passi (1972) observed significant developmental trends of creativity scores along grades nineth through eleventh. Similar results were obtained by Venkatarami Reddy and Balakrishna Reddy (1984) and Venkatarami Reddy and Saleena (1988).

Venkateswara Rao (1987) found that increase in age was accompanied by increase in creative performance. 13-14 years age could be considered as the critical period where creative performance is in full bloom and increase in sequential grades showed increase in creative performance.

Olshin (1965) found a significant positive relationship between age and verbal creativity test scores but the relationship did not hold for non-verbal? tasks.

Similarly Dharmagandans (1981) study revealed that both 14 year and 15 year old children scored significantly better than 13 year old children in general. But in the case of verbal tests the difference between 14 year and 15 year old children was significant. 15 year old children scored significantly better than 14 year old children.

Contradictions in the research findings exist in this area also. While the studies cited above indicate a positive relation between creativity and age, as early as in 1906 Colvin and Meyer found, on the basis of compositions written by children from grades three through twelve, a general decline in imagination with age.

Passi (1972) and Thamma Prateep (1976) also observed that there was a negative relationship between age and creativity.

Vohra (1975) found that there was a significant negative correlation between the age of the students and their non-verbal creativity among primary school students. Singh (1978) obtained a similar result with teacher trainees.

Raina (1970) found that the relationship between age and fluency was negative and significant, while it was not significant in the case of age and flexibility.

Ruth and Birren (1985) observed a decline in creativity with age, which they attributed to reduce speed of information processing, a lower level of complexity and decreased willingness to risk original solutions.

Some studies reported sex differences in the effect of age on creativity. Rawat and Agarwal (1977) for example found that upto 13 years of age boys were more creative than girls but after that there was a consistent downward trend in the creativity of boys, where as girls score was found gradual increase with age.

There were also some studies which reported no effect of age on creativity. For example Iscoe and Pierce Jones (1963) found no significant age changes in ideational fluency using the unusual uses task with black and white children, 5 to 9 years of age. Jain (1975) Rasool (1977) and Bhargava (1977) also found that there was no relationship between creativity and age.

Creativity and Locality

As early as in 1969 a study was conducted by Aaron, Marihal and Malatesha in which they explored the differences in creativity among rural and urban students. These investigators found no significant difference in the creativity of the two groups.

Singh (1981) Joshi (1982) and Chandrakant (1987) also found that there was no significant difference in the creativity of urban and rural students.

In a study on the creativity of teacher trainees from urban and rural areas. Jayaswal (1977) reported no significant difference between the two groups.

However, Sharma (1971, 1972, 1974) reported that rural students were significantly more creative than urban students. Sehgal (1978) also reported the similar results.

On the other hand Passi (1971) observed that urban students were significantly more creative than rural students. Singh (1979) found that urban residential background were more conducive for creativity than rural residential backgrounds. It was observed that in a creative group 89% of the subjects were of urban backgrounds while 11% were of rural backgrounds. Studies conducted by Singh (1977) Singh (1978) and Srivastava (1978) also reported superiority of urban students over rural students in creativity.

Dharmagandan (1981) reported that urban students scored significantly higher than rural students on flexibility and originality measures of verbal and non-verbal creativity.

According to Agarwal and Gupta (1982) locality plays a significant role in developing creative potential among the students. Their findings did of discriminate between residing in homes and those residing in hostels.

The study of Jayaswal (1977) Singh (1981), Joshi (1982) Rajasekhar Reddy (1977) on teacher trainees also reported no significant difference in the creativity scored of the teacher trainees belonging to the urban and rural areas.

Creativity and Birth Order

What is the relationship between birth order and creativity? Unfortunately, there appears to be little consensus as to what this relationship is most of the research in the area was indirectly focused on family influences and child rearing practices (Getzels and Dillon, 1973).

Eisenman and Schussel (1970) have concluded that later born males are significantly less creative than the first born males on the three measures of creativity used (complexity preference, personal opinion survey, unusual uses.).

Similarly, Srivastava (1977) found that first borns scored higher on creativity tests compared to later borns.

Jarial (1978) conducted a study to findout the differences in creativity among first borns and later borns and found that first borns were superior on different components of verbal creativity.

In another study conducted by Jarial (1982) to compare the fluency, flexibility, originality and total creativity scores of the students of different birth orders first, second, third, fourth, fifth, sixth and seventh on a sample of 600 male and female students of classes IX, X and XI studying in various educational institution of Indore city, it was found that (i) Students who were first born scored significantly higher than those who were second, third, fourth, fifth, sixth and seventh borns in originality, they scored better on fluency and total creativity than third, fourth, fifth and sixth borns, they were better than fourth and fifth borns in flexibility. (2) Second borns were significantly higher than the fourth and fifth borns in fluency, they were better than fifth borns in flexibility, originality and total creativity. (3) Third borns were significantly better than those whose birth order was five with regard to fluency flexibility, originality and total creativity. (4) Those whose birth order was four scored significantly higher than students whose birth order was five in originality and total creativity measures. (5) Seventh borns were significantly higher than fifth borns in flexibility.

Jarial and Sharma (1980) reviewed 3 studies investigating the relationship between creativity and birth order and concluded that the studies indicated a significant superiority of first borns over the later borns.

Comeae (1980) compared scores on the TTCT of 32 sets of first and second born siblings. The older siblings and significantly higher scores on the fluency, originality and elaboration sub-tests, but not on the flexibility sub-test.

Daved (1980) also found that the first borns were more creative than those who were later born. Chandrakant (1987) also obtained similar results.

First or last born secondary school students (aged 13-16 years) compelled the three verbal subtests of the passi test of creativity. First borns scored significantly higher on fluency, flexibility, originality and total score than last born Ss (Jarial, 1982).

Eiseman (1988) in his study on creativity, birth order and risk taking on 100 first born and 100 later born adult males found that risk taking and creativity were related and that both were associated with birth order.

Contrary to the above findings, Staffieri (1970) found that later borns scored higher on the two creativity measures he used, Viz, word association test, unusual uses test.

Bliss (1970) who studied 74 creative writers also found a slight predominance from the second half of siblings.

Srivastava (1977) conducted on investigation to findout the relationship between creativity and number of siblings and found that there was no significant different in the creativity scores of the students belonging to different birth order groups.

Badrinath and Satyanarayanan (1979) also found that first, second, third and fourth borns did not differ significantly with respect to their creativity scores.

Kaur (1986) also reported that creative abilities were found to be independent of birth order. Datta (1968) Harnek and Manjit (1988) Venkata Rami Reddy and Tulasi Devi (1988) also obtained similar results.

Creativity and Annual Income

Many studies have reported that creativity comes from high socio economic status families. Jarial (1979) found that students belonging to higher than the students of upper middle, lower middle and low socio economic status groups on creativity tests. Students belonging to upper middle socio economic status scored significantly higher than students of low socio economic status and the students of lower middle socio economic status scored significantly higher than student of low economic status on creativity.

Ranjana Pandit and Katiyar (1976) found that creativity was positively and significantly related to level of adjustment, level of socio economic status and level of scholastic achievement.

Zargar and Neelamdhar (1988) observed that students belonging to parents of high socio economic status were more creative than those of parents of low economic status for both the sexes.

Ahmed (1980) found that there was a significant difference in the verbal and non-verbal creativity of the students coming from advantaged and disadvantaged home backgrounds favouring the former.

Awasthy (1979) found that students of very high socio economic status were superior to the student belonging to high, average and low strata in flexibility, originality and total creativity, while the students of high socio economic status were superior to the students of very high, average and low strata in fluency. The students of high socio economic status were superior to the students of low socio economic status in total creativity and the students of very high socio economic status were superior to the students of low and average socio economic status in fluency.

Sharma (1980) found that students of high socio-economic status scored significantly higher than students of low socio economic status in originality and total creativity. Where as it had no effect on fluency and flexibility components. Sharma and Jarial (1980) observed that students of high socio-economic status scored significantly higher than students of low socio-economic status in fluency.

Singh and Katiyar (1977) observed that students of low socio economic status were higher than those belonging to middle and high socio economic status in all the areas of creativity. The populars of high socio-economic status were higher than the populars of middle socio-economic status in all the areas of creativity. The mean score in all areas of creativity of isolates was positively and significantly related to socio economic status.

However, Seetharam and Vedanayagam (1979) reported that there was no significant difference in the creativity scores of high, middle and low socio economic students.

Badrinath and Satyanarayana (1979) also did not find significant difference in the creativity scores of the students of high, middle and low socio-economic status.

Similarly Sharma and Jarial (1981) observed that there was no significant difference in the creativity of the students of high and low socio-economic status.

Vohra (1975) stated that the correlation between socio economic status and non-verbal creativity indicated that these two variables were not significantly correlated.

Dutt (1988) found that the total verbal creativity was not found to be related significantly to socio-economic status.

Rawat and Agarwal (1977) found no significant difference in the creativity scores of the students of business and non business communities and except in higher income group. Social class as such was found to play no role in creative thinking.

Creativity and Achievement Motivation

Girijest Kumar (1978) found that high creative were more achievement motivated than low creative.

Achievement motivation in relation to other variables was studied by Sudhir (1989). It was found that pupils having low self-reliance and higher mean motivation scores than those having high self reliance. It was also found that persons who were more free from cognitive disturbances, like nervous feeling, were more achievement oriented.

Mcclelland (1956) explored the relationship between creativity and achievement motivation. He found that successful scientists like successful salesmen or business entrepreneurs, had a higher need for achievement, because high motivation predisposes him to take moderate calculated risks in which the success or failure of the enterprise depends upon his own efforts.

Torrance (1964) surveyed a large number of studies and compiled a set of characteristics found in one or more studies to differentiate highly creative persons from less creative ones. He found that creative people had a desire to excel.

Helson (1966) conducted a study on 135 women who were nominated by the faculty. She found creative women to have a greater need for autonomy, a lesser need for acting an impulse and a stronger motivation to take creative role.

Khatena and Torrance (1977) administered from I and II of the onematopoeia and images test and the runner studies of attitude patterns to college junior subjects were divided into high, middle and low groups in terms of their originality scores, based on their performance on onematopoeia and images tests. The analysis elicited that high group in originality tended to be freedom and achievement oriented on the runners test.

Raina (1970) in his study on teachers under training found that the high creative students as compared to low creatives, were significantly higher on creative motivation. The low creative group was significantly higher than the high creative group on critical motivation. There was no significant difference between the two groups on power motivation.

Singh (1972) administered a creativity test specifically designed for his study and achievement motivation scale by Mukherjee to 239 students, out of whom 131 were boys and 108 were girls. High creative and low creative groups were identified by selecting 18% top and 18% bottom scores on creativity test separately, in the groups of boys and girls. The analysis of high and low creative boys as well as high and low creative girls indicated no statistically significant difference between the high and the low creative groups of each sex, through high creative groups had some what higher achievement motivation. Comparison between high creative boys and girls revealed no statistically significant difference between each of the groups, but the boys tended to have higher need for achievement.

Jha (1975) conducted a study on 534 students of IX, X and XI grades in which she administered Torrance tests of creativity junior, senior high school personality Inventory. Singh's Interest Reward, etc., the sample was divided into four groups namely high creative boys, high creative girls, low creative boys and low creative girls. The results suggested that achievement motivation was positively related to creativity.

Creativity and Personality Factors

Creative Performance does not depend on certain cognitive characteristics and operations. Realising the importance of non cognitive characteristics Guilford (1976) proposed that consideration be given to what motivates individuals in terms of needs interests and attitudes that help the individuals to be productive and creative. Roe (1951) also suggested that personality factors are crucial in the development of creativity.

The personality characteristics of creative children have been studied in a variety of ways—biographical and autobiographical reports of eminent adults interviews with the mothers and teachers of creative children, interviews with the children themselves self administered inventories and various tests and procedures designed to differentiate the creative child from the less creative one. However developmental trends have not been studied. Indeed most investigations imply that the character traits reported are consistent from early childhood. The resulting composite picture of the creative child in terms of personality is therefore a blurred and somewhat incongruent one (Arasteh and Arasteh 1976).

Various authors have argued that creativity is related to unique cognitive factors (Guilford 1950 Lowerfied, 1957) and what is dependent upon certain personality characteristics (Freud, 1949; Barren, 1965, Couch and Keniston, 1960 Mc Guire, 1960).

Bhattacharya (1956) observed that high creative possessed shallow feeling for life, high sensitivity and ability for prelogical thinking. In 1960, he found that 'born creative' were introverts while 'acquired creative' were extroverts. Roy Choudhary (1962, 1965 and 1966) reported that high creative were more distinctly marked by their emotional and temperamental traits than by cognitive and motivational aspects of their personality. Raina (1968) reported that high creatives were characterized by greater achievement, autonomy, change and endurance. Ahmed (1969) found that originals were more dominant than unoriginal while with regard to the rest of the dimensions of personality no significant differences were observed.

Aaron and Malatesha (1972) stated that high creative were highly motivated, less modern but more conservative. Bhan (1972) reported that none of the factors of sociability was related to the creative potential. Later in 1973, he reported that level of aspiration of high creatives was high but it was within the productive resources of these individuals.

Verma (1973) reported that traits of autonomy, non confirmity and openness of mind were functionally related to the abilities of divergent thinking. Rehman and Hussain (1973) found a negative and significant relationship between social desirability and verbal fluency, non-verbal elaboration total verbal creativity and total non-verbal creativity. The relationship between social desirability and non-verbal flexibility and non-verbal originality was also negative but insignificant. Lalithamma (1973) found that creativity was positively and significantly correlated with positive self concept, intelligence and negative aesthetic self concept.

According to Joshi (1974) there was no significant correlation between creativity scores and different personality factors except

Factor-B (general intelligence versus mental defect), Factor-G (character or super ego strength versus lack of rigid internal standard) Factors-I (previsia versus Harria) Factor-Q2 (Radicalism versus conservatism of temperament) Factor-Q3(high self sentiment of formation) and Factor-Q4 (high energic tension versus low energic tension). High creative possessed social boldness, high self sentiment and high guilt proneness (Goyal, 1974).

Paramesh and Narayanan (1974) reported that high creative were significantly higher than low creative with respect to their interest in persuasive, linguistic, artistic and musical interest areas. In another study the authors found that high creative had a lower level of sociable tendency than low creative. High creative were found to enjoy relatively less in the company of others, experienced difficulty in making friends, and were less sympathetic than low creative counter parts on active, vigorous, impulsive, dominant, stable and reflective traits of temperament. Chawla (1976) reported that high creative were more sober and more intelligent than low creative. According to Nair (1976) creative were characterised by high self reliance, sense of personal worth, sense of personal freedom, feeling of belongingness, freedom from withdrawing tendencies, freedom from nervous symptoms, more social standards, more social skills, more involved in family relations, school relations and community relations.

Chauhan (1971) Kumar (1981) Srivastava (1978) Gulats (1979) and Verma (1980) found that creativity was positively and significantly related to intoversion, while Nagia (1977) and Bhargava (1979) found that creativity was negatively related with extroversion. Gopal (1975) observed that creative science students were more reserved emotionally stable, assertive, sober, expedient, venturesome, suspicious, imaginative, shrewd, experimenting, self sufficient and relaxed than engineering students. The non creative science students when compared with science creative students were found to be more outgoing, affected by feelings, humble, happy go lucky, conscientious, shy, trusting, practical, conservative, group dependent and tense.

According to Singh, Mathur and Saxena (1977) high creative felt more secure than non-creative. High creative were found to possess rational optimism, high ego, strength, realistic and healthy attitude towards life, openness to experience, dedicated persistence, sense of worth assertiveness, self confidence and self actualization (Jha 1975), and they were more conscientious and persistent, more undemonstrative, inactive and phlegmatic than low creative (Kaur, 1978). Creative were found to be more intelligent, emotionally stable, venturesome, self assured, undisciplined, and relaxed (Singh, 1978).

In a factor analytical study of specific personality characteristics and creativity, creativity was grouped with characteristics like curiousity and initiative which showed that the personality of a creative child was similar to that of a creative adult (Upadhyaya, 1982).

Sansanwal and Jarial (1979) reported that creative were more intelligent, happy go lucky, impulsive, lively, relaxed, easy to get on with, tranquil, torpid and unfrustated. They were also outgoing, warm hearted and participating, emotionally mature, stable and realistic about life (Sansanwal and Jarial, 1979). They were self sufficient resourceful, preferring their own decision, self controlled, self disciplined and had high self concept (Verma,1979).

Dasgupta (1977) reported that as compared to low creative, the high creative suffered more from parental relationship, were more involved and non-conformist in their beliefs and attitudes, psychotic and neurotic tendencies were more prominent in high creative; they possessed high self concept (Gupta, 1977 and Singh, 1978) less achievement motivation (Lal and Chilana, 1977); and high intelligence, more social boldness, stronger self-sentiment and less tension (Mallappa and Upadhyana, 1977).

Srinivasan (1984) investigated the disposition toward originality in 110 male industries supervisors all of whom were engineers. They were administered a battery of tests that include the unusual uses subtlest of Torrance test of creative thinking. Rorschach inkblot test, test of Consequence, Thematic apperception, word rearrangement and Eysencks personality inventory. Results showed that more creative Ss exhibited qualities of extroversion has similar degrees of neuroticism as Ss who wireless creative and had low psychotic tendencies.

Bhargava (1979) found that creativity was negatively and significantly related to anxiety, extraversion and was positively and significantly related to independence. Sharma (1979) stated that fluent students were found to be initiative good observers, adventurous, sensitive, less contended in needs, relaxed, curious and desirous to do high acts with sincerity. The flexible students were found to be fault finders, adventurous interested in various types of activities. The original students were found to be independent, desirous to do unique things, self confident.

Gulati (1979) reported that the respect to different components of creativity, viz., fluency, flexibility, and originality, introverts performed better than extroverts. But in some other studies, it was observed that introverts did not differ significantly from extroverts in fluency, flexibility and originality (Jarial, 1980 and Jarial and Sharma, 1981). High creative possessed greater sense of humour, and less conformity than low creative (Gupta, 1979).

Pandy (1980) found that in comparison to the non creative male pupil teachers, the creative male pupil teachers were found to be good natured, easy going, emotionally expressive, ready to cooperate, unconventional and inadequate. Creative female teachers were fast learners, tended to grasp ideas quickly, self assured, independent minded, sociable, bold, ready to try new things, imaginative, interested in intellectual matters and fundamental issues. Misra (1980) stated that both flexible and non flexible teachers were emotional nature, realistic about life, possessing ego strength, assertive, self assured, independent minded, extra punitive, disregarding authority, dominated by a sense of duty, playful, responsible, conscientious, moralistic, sociable, bold, ready to try new things, spontaneous, careless of details.

Jyotsna (1980) found that high creative students tend to be more reserved, critical, more intelligent, more self reliant, higher super ego strength and less frustrated than their less creative counterparts. Super ego strength was found to be a positive correlate of creativity in the case of total sample.

Kaur (1980) found that creativity was positively and significantly related with positive intelligence self concept, positive character self concept, positive aesthetic self concept, positive adjustment self concept. Self concept intelligence, self concept character and self concept adjustment. Lidhoo and Zargar (1980) found that creativity was negatively related to neuroticism. Singh (1980) reported that creativity was not related to the level of aspirations and frustration reactions. Kumar (1981) reported that high creative were less anxious than their low creative counterparts, high creative children were significantly more extrovert than the low creatives.

Singh and Mehra (1981) found that high creative preferred unconventional occupations as air hostess, lawyers and scientists, where as low creative preferred conventional occupations as teacher. Further low creative were more aspirants than high creative.

Jarial and Sharma, (1981) found that there was no significant difference in the fluency, flexibility, originality and total creativity scores of introvert and extrovert students. Brooder Singh (1980, 1986) found that biographical and personality factors affect the development of creativity. The interaction effects of biographical factors and personality factors on creativity have been neglected by most of the researchers in the past. The effect of biographical factors on creativity can be minimised but can not be ignored completely.

Kundu (1987) observed that creativity was positively related to psychoticism, while the relationship between creativity and extroversion was curvilinear. Dysthemics were found to be more creative than hysterics. Chadha (1987) found that there was a positive and significant relationship between creativity and factor 'G' (expedient versus conscientious) creativity and factor Q2 (group dependent versus self sufficient).

Geetha Cheubey (1989) observed that creativity is positively correlated with self confidence, withdrawing tendencies and emotional instability.

There seems to be much similarity in the characteristics of creative persons enlisted by different reaches even though the ideal creative personality differs from culture to culture, as indicated by Torrance cross cultural study (Torrance, 1965).

Paramesh (1970) found the creative children to be neither extrovert not introvert. They were neither high nor low on neuroticism and anxiety. On the contrary he found them to be stable in personality organisation and characterized by high theoretical and aesthetic values.

Goyal (1972) emphasized that high creative children at school stage possess a high level of energy reject repression and suppression for the control of their impulses. They are more introvert and independent in thought and action and have open minds. They can tolerate ambiguity and entertain opposing values.

Kumar (1978) stated that the high creative individuals were introvert in Comparison to low creative individuals. High creative individuals were significantly higher on theoretical and aesthetic values as compared to low creative individuals and they were more achievement motivated than the low creative. Kumar (1978) examined personality patterns of high and low creative children and found that high creative as differentiated from low creative were more conscientious and persistent (G^{+}) and undemonstrative, inactive and phlegmatic (D-1). On the other hand the low creative were expedient(G-1) and excitable (D^{+1}). Science students were found to be significantly out scoring than humanities students on flexibility dimension of creativity. No significant mean differences were observed between the two groups in fluency, originality and elaboration dimensions.

Singh (1977) reported that high creativity among student teachers tended to go with higher economic value, better personality adjustment, better family background and urban living. Low creativity on the other hand seemed to be associated with higher theoretical value, adjustment, poorer family background and rural living.

Singh (1980) found that the creative were significantly higher than non-creative in economic value. On the other hand non creative were significantly higher than creative in theoretical value. There was no significant difference in the aesthetic social, political and religious values of the creative and non creative student teachers.

On the basis of the observations noticed in the related literature with regard to the conceptualisation of creativity, its measurement, the related variables etc., the researcher stated the problem for his research with its objectives, hypotheses and variables included in the investigation in the succeeding chapter.

3

Statement of the Problem, Objectives, Hypothesis and Variables

SIGNIFICANCE OF THE PROBLEM

Education in our country does no good in any qualitative aspect. Teaching emphasises on drill and grill in the acquisition of new data and in their utilization. According to Bloom (1958) there is some reason to believe that education system can reduce originality and creativity. This negative effect on creativity is mostly marked when examinations, instructional materials and processes all emphasize learning by rote and the goal is centred on getting through the examinations. Any novel class room situation occurs only accidentally and not by any design. Though the topic creativity was recently introduced in the teacher training courses most of the teachers are ignorant of the concept of creativity.

Universalization of Elementary Education (UEE) has always been a matter of great concern for policy makers in India. While considerable progress has been made as a consequence of inputs provided under various schemes during the last five decades the target of achieving UEE has still remained a distant dream. The most significant reasons for the task remaining unfinished have been disregard to the element of Contextuality and a misplaced emphasis on uniform prescription for bringing about qualitative improvement in primary education.

An evaluation of the outcome of learning in school has therefore, tended to emphasize knowledge, comprehension, understanding critical acumen, intelligence, ability etc. It is only lately with the rapid developments in science and technology, that creativity and its study has become important. It is now realized that any system of education in a society should encourage creativity so that a society can be saved from stagnation and the individual can also have his own fulfilment. Thus we find that creativity is entering into the curriculum of a school as well as in its evaluation. Studies are being made about the nature of creativity, how can it be nurtured, what instruction can help its development, how it can be measured and predicted and so on.

The aim of education is to develop an integrated personality suitably stuffed and equipped all its dimensions, viz. physical, mental, moral, emotional and vocational. Education does not mean imparting of verbal knowledge. The knowledge that is gathered in schools, should be capable of being used for all life situations, service to society and helping to improve the deplorable conditions of one's own country. The characteristics of true education is humility apart from developing intelligence, skills, power of discrimination and creativity.

STATEMENT OF THE PROBLEM

In the light of the review of literature and keeping in view the importance of the teacher in developing the creative thinking among learners, the problem for the research is stated below.

The Title of the Problem is *Creativity: Its Correlates of Certain Personal, Social and Psychological Variables of Student Teachers of DIETs.*

OBJECTIVES OF THE STUDY

1. To study the level of creativity among student teachers of DIET.
2. To study the influence of personal and social variable on creativity.
3. To study the influence of psychological variables on creativity.
4. To Predict creativity with the help of a selected bunch of independent variables.

HYPOTHESIS

1. The general level of creativity among student teachers of DIETs is normal.
2. The personal and demographic variables of student teachers of DIETs would not bring any significant influence on their creativity (each variable will be tested independently).
3. The psychological variables such as achievement motivation, scientific attitude, and 16 personality factors of student teachers of DIETs would not significantly influence their creativity (each variable will be tested independently).
4. It would not be possible to predict creativity (verbal, non-verbal or both) with the help of personal, social and psychological variables.

VARIABLES STUDIED

The dependent variable in the study is creativity of student teachers of DIETs. The independent variables are broadly grouped under personal, social and psychological variables.

The following definitions, descriptions are operationalised for the purpose of measuring the variables in the study.

Creativity: Creative thinking is judged on the basis of the verbal and non-verbal creativity scores obtained on all the components of creativity fluency, flexibility, and originality.

Verbal Creativity

1. Verbal fluency is the ability to produce many ideas for a given task.
2. Verbal flexibility is the ability to produce ideas that show a person's movement from one level of thinking to another or shifts in thinking.
3. Verbal originality is the ability to produce ideas that not many people think of or that are unusual, remote and clever.
4. Total verbal creativity is judged on the basis of the total

scores obtained on all the three dimensions of verbal creativity i.e., fluency, flexibility and originality scores.

Non-verbal Creativity

1. Non-verbal fluency is the ability to produce many ideas for a given task.
2. Non-verbal flexibility is the ability to produce ideas that show a persons movement from one level of thinking to another, or shifts in thinking.
3. Non-verbal originality is the ability to produce ideas that not many people think of or that are unusual, remote and clever.
4. Total non-verbal creativity is judged on the basis of the total score obtained on all the three dimensions of Non-verbal creativity (fluency, flexibility and originality) scores.

Composite Creativity (Verbal and Non-verbal)

Composite creativity is judged on the basis of the creativity scores obtained on all the different components of creativity i.e., verbal and non-verbal.

Composite fluency is judged on the basis of the scores obtained on the verbal fluency and non-verbal fluency.

Composite flexibility is judged on the basis of the scores obtained on the verbal flexibility and non-verbal flexibility.

Composite originality is judged on the basis of the scores obtained on the verbal originality and non-verbal originality.

Total Composite creativity is judged on the basis of the creativity scores obtained on all the three components—fluency, flexibility and originality on both verbal and non-verbal tests.

Sex

Student Teachers of DIETs of both the sexes are included in the study to find out whether there is any significant difference between male and female student teachers in the level of their creativity.

Education Qualification

The student teachers of DIETs were divided into two groups on the basis of their qualifications as those who are suitably qualified i.e. with intermediate qualifications and those who are over qualified i.e., with first degree or above qualifications.

Age

With regard to age the sample of student teachers of DIETs was divided into three groups on the basis of their age viz., (i) upto twenty years (ii) 21-23 years (iii) 24 and above years.

Birth Order

The sample of student teachers of DIETs were divided into three groups on the basis of their birth order (i) 1st born (ii) 2nd born (iii) later born.

Locality

The entire sample of student teachers of DIETs was drawn from the localities viz: Rural and Urban.

Family Literacy Index

The total sample of student teachers of DIETs was divided into three groups on the basis of their family literacy index viz: (i) Low (0-5) (ii) moderate (6-10) (iii) High (11 and above).

Occupational Status of the Father

Sample of student teachers of DIETs was divided into three groups on the basis of the occupation of the father viz., (i) Labour (ii) Agriculture (iii) Secured job.

Annual Income

With regard to Annual Income of the family the sample of student teachers of DIETs was divided into three groups viz., (i) 1-10 thousands (ii) 11-50 thousands (iii) 51 thousand and above.

Achievement Motivation

Achievement motivation is expectancy of finding satisfaction in mastery of difficult and challenging performances where as in the field of education in particular, it stands for the pursuit of excellence.

Scientific Attitude

In this investigation the word attitude is used to refer to 'a mental and neutral state of readiness, organised through experience, exerting a directive or a dynamic influence upon the individual responses to subjects and situations with which it is related.

On attitude towards ideas and information and particular ways of evaluation of them, a formulation which distinguishes it from an attitude to science or scientists on the one hand and from an ability to carryout scientific procedures on the other.

Sixteen Personality Factors

Factor A: Reserved, detached, critical, cool vs outgoing warm hearted easy going participating.

The person who scores low on factor A tends to be stiff, cool, skeptical and alone. He likes things rather than people, working alone, and avoidence of clash of view points. He/She is likely to be precise and rigid in his way of doing things and in personal standards and in many occupations these are desirable taints. He may tend at times, to be critical, obstructive or hard.

The person who scores high on factor 'A' tends to be matured, easy going emotionally expressive ready to cooperative, attentive to people, soft hearted, kindly and adaptable. He likes occupations dealing with people and socially impressive situation. He readily forms active groups. He is generous in personal relations, less afraid of criticism better able to remember names of people.

Factor B: Less intelligence, concrete thinking vs more intelligent, abstract thinking.

The person scoring low on Factor-B tends to be slow to learn and grasp, dull and sluggish. He tends to hero have little capacity for the higher forms of knowledge and to be some what boorish. His dullness may be simply a reflection of low intelligence or it may represent for functioning due to psycho lpathology.

The person who scores high on factor-B tends to be quick to grasp ideas, as fast learner, intelligent. There is some correlation with the level of culture and some what alertness. High score indicates deterioration of mental functions in pathological conditions.

Factor-C: Affected by feeling, emotionally less stable vs emotionally stable, calm, mature.

The person scores low on Factor-C tends to be low frustration, tolerance for unsatisfactory conditions changeable, evading necessary reality demands, neurotically fatigued, worrying, easily annoyed. Generally dissatisfied having neurotic symptoms (phobias, sleep disturbances, psychosomatic complaints etc). Low score on Factor-C is common to almost all forms of neurotic and mental disorders.

The person who scores high on Factor-C tends to be emotionally mature, stable, calm, realistic about life, unruffled possessing ego strength, having an integrated philosophy of life, better able to maintain high group and morale. Sometimes he may be a person making a resigned adjustment to unsolved emotional problems.

Factor-E: Humble, mild, accommodating i.e., submissive vs assertive, independent, aggressive, i.e., dominance.

The person who scores on Factor-E tends to be dependent, a follower, and to take action, which goes along with the group. He is often soft hearted expressive and easily upset. This positivity is part of many neurotic syndromes.

The person who scores high on Factor-E tends to be assertive, self assumed, independent minded, bold his approach to situations. He may at times be hard, a low to himself, hostile, though minded, authoritarian (managing others) and disregards authority.

Factor-F: Sober, prudent, serious, i.e., disurgency vs Happy-go-lucky, gay, enthusiastic i.e., surgency.

The person who scores low on Factor F tends to be restrained reticent, introspective. He is sometimes in communicative, pessimistic, noxious and considered to be sung. He tends to be sober, dependable person.

The person who scores high on this trait tends to be cheerful, active, talkative, frank, expressive, quick, alert, unperturbable. He is frequently chosen as an elected leader. He may be impulsive and mercurial.

Factor-G: Expedient, evades rules, i.e., weaker super ego strength vs. conscientious preserving, rule bound i.e., stronger super ego strength.

The person who scores low on factor-G tends to be steady in purpose. He is often casual and lacking in effort for group undertakings and cultural demands his freedom from group influence may lead to anti-social acts, but at times, make him more effective, while his refusal, to be bound by rules causes him to have less somatic upset from stress.

The person who scores high on Factor-G tends to be strong in character, preserving, responsible, determined, consistent, planful, energetic, cautious, well organised. He is usually conscientious or moralistic and he prefers hard working people to witty companions. The inner categorical imperative of this essential super ego (in the psycho analytical sense) should be distinguished from the superficially similar social ideal self of Q_3+.

Factor-H: Shy, restrained, timid i.e., Threctia Vs Venturesome, Socially bold i.e., parnia.

The person who scores low on this traits tends to be say, withdrawing, cautious, retiring, cooling, a well flower. He usually has inferiority feelings. He tends to be slow and impeded in speech in expressing himself, dislikes occupations with personal contacts, prefers one or two close friends to large groups, and is not given to keeping in contact with all that is going on around him.

The person who scores high on factor-H tends to be sociable, bold, ready to try new things, a spontaneous and abundant in emotional response. His thick skinnedness enables him to face wear and tear in dealing with people and gruelling emotional situations without fatigue. However he can be careless of detail, ignore danger signals, and consume much time. He tends to be "Pushy" and actively interested in the opposite sex.

Factor-I: Tough minded, self reliant i.e., Harria vs. Tenderminded, dependent, sensitive i.e., premsia.

The person who scores low on Factor-I tends to be practically realistic, masculine, independent, responsible, but skeptical or subjective and uncultured. He is some times unmoved, hard, cynical, smug. He tends to keep group operating on a practical and realistic non-sense basis.

The person who scores high on this trait tends to be tender minded, day dreaming, artistically fastidious. He is some times demanding of attention and help, impatient, dependent, impractical. He dislikes crude people and rough occupations. He tends to slow up group performance and to upset group morals by unrealistic fussiness.

Factor-L: Trusting adaptable, free of jealousy i.e., Alaxia vs. Suspicious self opinionated hard to tool i.e., protection.

The person who scores low on Factor-L tends to be free of jealous tendencies, adaptable, cheerful, uncompetitive, concerned about other people, a good team-worker.

The person who scores high on Factor-L tends to be mistrusting and doubtful. He is often involved in his own ego, is self opinionated and interested in internal mental life. He is usually deliberate in his actions, unconcerned about other people, a poor team member.

Factor-M: Practical, careful, conventional, i.e., Prexernia vs. Imaginative, wrapped up in inner urgencies i.e., Austia.

The person who scores low on Factor-M tends to be anxious to do the right things, attentive to practical matters, and subject to the dedications of what is obviously possible. He is concerned over detail, able to keep his head in emergencies, but sometimes unimaginative, and narrowly correct.

The person who scores high on Factor-M tends to be unconventional, unconcerned over every matters Bohemian, self motivated, ego centric, sensitive, imaginative. He some times makes emotional scores is somewhat irresponsible, impractical, undependable. He is often rejected in group situations.

Factor-N: Forthright, natural, artless, i.e., Artlessness vs. Shrwed, calculating worldly i.e., Shrewdness.

The person who scores low in Factor-N tends to be unsophisticated, sentimental and simple. He is sometimes crude and awkward, but easily pleased and content with what comes, and is natural and spontaneous.

The person who scores high on this trait tends to be polished, experienced, wild, shrewd. He is often hard-headed and analytical. He has an intellectual unsentimental approach to situations approach akin to cynicism.

Factor-O: Placid, self assumed, confident i.e., untroubled, adequacy vs. Apprehensive worrying, depressive, troubled i.e., guilt proneness.

The person who scores low in Factor-O tends to be placid, calm, with unshakable nerve. He has a mature, unaxious confidence in himself and his capacity to deal with things. He is resident and secure.

The person who scores high of Factor-O tends to be depressed, moody, a worried, suspicious, good in avoiding people. He has a child like tendency to anxiety in difficulties. He does not feel accepted in groups of free to participate. High Factor-O score is very common in clinical groups of all types.

Factor-Q_1: Conservative, tolerant of traditional difficulties i.e., conservatism Vs Experimenting Critical, free thinking i.e., Radicalism.

The person who scores low on Factor-Q_1, tends to be overly cautious and moderate. He is opposed to any change, inclined to go along with traditions and tends not to be interested in analytical "intellectual" thought.

The person who scores high on Factor-Q_1 tends to be interested in intellectual matters and has doubts on fundamental issues. He frequently takes issues with ideas, either old or new. He tends to be well informed, less inclined to moralise, more inclined to experiment in life, generally and more tolerant of inconvenience and change.

Factor Q_2: Ground independent, sound follower, i.e., group adherence Vs. self sufficient, resourceful i.e., self sufficiency.

The person who scores low on factor Q_2 prefers to work and make decisions with other people and depends on social approval and administration. He tends to go along with the group and may be lacking in individual resolution. He is not necessarily gregarious by choice, rather he needs group support.

The person who scores high on factor-Q_2 is temperamentally independent, accustomed to go his own way, making decisions and taking action on his own. He discounts public opinion, but is not necessarily dominant in his relation with others. He does not dislike people but simply does not mind their agreement or support.

Factor-Q_3: Undisciplined, self-conflict, careless i.e., low integration Vs. controlled, socially precise following self-image, i.e., high self-concept control.

The person who scores low on factor-Q_3 will not be bothered with will-control and regard for social demands. He is not over considerable, careful or pains-taking. He may feel mal-adjusted and may show maladjustment.

The person who scores high on Factor-Q_3 tends to have strong control of his emotions and general behaviour, is inclined to be socially aware and careful and evidence what is commonly termed 'self-respect' and regard for social reputation. He sometimes tends, however to be obstinate. Effective leaders and some paranoids are high on Q_3.

Factor Q_4: Relaxed, tranquil, unfrustrated i.e., low ergic tension Vs. Tense, frustrated, driven i.e., high ergic tension.

The person who scores low on factor-Q_4 tends to be sedate, relaxed, composed and satisfied (not frustrated). In some situations, his over-satisfaction can lead to laziness and low performance in the sense that low motivation produces little trial and error conversely high tension level may disrupt school and work performance.

The person who scores high on factor-Q_4 tends to be tense, excitable, restless, fruitful, impatient. He is often fatigued, but unable to remain inactive. In groups he takes a poor view of the degree of unity, orderliness and leadership.

To realise the objectives, it is necessary to test the hypotheses by employing appropriate statistical tools in analyzing the quantitative data collected empirically through the relevant tools administered on a randomly selected sample of subjects. All these stages and steps of the investigation forms the methodology which is presented entitle in the next chapter.

4

Methodology

This chapter describes different methods employed in measuring the variables, selecting the sample, collecting the data, scoring and responses and analysing the data thus obtained.

MEASUREMENT OF THE VARIABLES

As disclosed in the earlier chapter the study aims at measuring the variables—both dependent and independent variables. To measure different kinds of variables it is necessary to identify appropriate sealing techniques to be used, type of items, response pattern, weightages to be assigned to the alternative responses etc. Some times the researcher may resort to use standardized tools developed by earlier researchers and in some occasions he/she may has to construct and develop a tool if suitable instrument is not available. Keeping these possibilities in view, the researcher, thoroughly reviewed different tools to measure the variables included in the present investigation and most acceptable decisions are taken.

Measurement of Creativity

As mentioned earlier, the theoretical frame work, for development of tests of creativity was provided by empirical studies on the nature of creativity. Especially useful in this context is the distinction Guilford has made between divergent thinking and convergent thinking abilities. Divergent thinking is a kind of mental process in which one thinks in different directions, unlike in convergent thinking which moves towards responses that suit the known and accepted is correct. Divergent thinking leads to novel responses to given stimuli. Its unique feature is that scope is provided to produce a variety of responses for any given stimuli.

The creativity of the subjects was measured in the present study with the help of a battery of creativity tests constructed in Telugu[1] by Venkatarami Reddy. The tests were developed in line with those of Guilford (1962). Gazelles and Jackson (1962). Torrance (1962), and Wallach and Kogan (1965). The items in the sub tests were chosen taking into consideration their familiarity and relevance to the population on which they were to be used. The items were selected in consultation with 6 judges, drawn from the Departments of Psychology and Education, who were conversant with creativity tests.

The battery of creativity tests used consisted of 10 sub tests. Seven of them were verbal tests while the remaining three were non-verbal tests. A brief description of the tests is presented in the following paragraphs.[2]

1. **Unusual Uses:** Basically the unusual uses test which is used in almost all creativity test batteries requires the subjects to redefine the object after thinking about the various ways in which it can be used. Common things like brick, wooden stick, water, and cotton were used as stimuli to let the subject's thinking go in different directions.

2. **Instances:** In this test the pupils were given 4 items for each of the items they were required to tell all things that suit the specific concept under question.

3. **Similarities:** The children were provided with 4 pairs of things and they were asked to suggest as many different ways in which the two things in a given pair of objects were similar. They were to generate various similarities between the two objects in each of the four pairs.

4. **Common Problems:** This test was designed to assess the ability of the subjects to see defects, needs and deficiencies. This is one of the tests of the factor termed 'sensitivity to problems' by Guilford (1951). The subjects were given 4 common situations and were

required to think of as many problems as they can, which they face in each of these situation.

5. **Impossibilities:** The impossibilities test is one involving complex restrictions and large potential. The task requires the children to think about all impossibilities (i.e.,) those which are beyond the capacity of the present day man-kind.

6. **Consequences:** In this test the subjects were confronted with certain hypothetical situations and they were required to think of all possible consequences of these hypothetical situations.

7. **Product Improvement:** The product improvement task is another complex task, which assess the ability of the subjects to think of different kinds of defects and ways of improving the given objects. They were given a list of 4 objects and asked to suggest as many ways of improving each of them. They were told not to worry about the practicability of the suggested improvement.

8. **Pattern Meanings:** This involved visual rather than verbal stimulus materials. The subjects were given 8 patterns and they were required to generate different possible meanings or interpretations for each of them and list out the different ways in which each looked like.

9. **Line Meanings:** This task contained eight figures each of which was continuous line of a particular sort. The subjects were to think of different interpretations appropriate to the form of each of the given lines. Each line was a single unit unlike the discrete elements that comprised the patterns in the pattern meaning test.

10. **Circles:** In this task the subjects were to construct meaningful figures with the given circles as base by drawing lines in side and or outside each of them. After completing each figure, they were required to name them.

Validity

According to Torrance (1962) perhaps one of the major reasons why research related to the measurement and development of creative thinking did not catch the imagination of educators in the past years lies in the failure of researchers to deal adequately with the difficult problems of criteria and validity. In the words of Taylor and Holland (1964) 'there is no more crucial problem in creativity than the criterion problem'. In the same way Arasteh and Arasteh (1976) opined that the crucial problems in creativity research are those of measurement and validity. Torrance (1962) observed that in most cases the theoretical rationale of the instruments developed 'made good sense' but their presumed validity was not convincing. Similarly Shapiro (1972) also commented that the problem of criterion represented the most challenging aspect of all researches into creativity.

Quite interestingly, the most careful jobs of criterion development have been done in connection with personality and life experience studies rather than in efforts to validate measures of the creative thinking abilities.

The gravity of the problem can be seen from the words of Khatena; "Measures of creativity originating from constructs whose complexities are better recognised than understood, have built in validation problems which the combined efforts of the university of Utah conferences (Taylor, 1956, 1957, 1959) and the critical and constructive evaluation directions by prominent men in the field (e.g. Mackler and Shontz, 1965, McNemar, 1964; Taylor, 1964; Wallach and Wing, 1963; Wallach and Kogan, 1965; Yamamoto, 1965) have to date could not resolve (Khatena, 1973).

At the second Minnesota conference on Gifted Children, Taylor (1960) listed the obstacles in identifying creative talent as follows.

1. Rarity of the highest type of creative thinking.
2. Failure of the society to recognise creative products until one or two generations after the creation.
3. Tendency in the society to reward recognised creative talents with promotions in to positions where the individuals are not able to continue their creative work.
4. The stress of academic programme of non-creative activities.

5. Failure of academic programme to reward creative achievement and divergent thinking.

At the 1959 Utah conference, Guilford discussed the validation process as a part of the report of the committee on predictors of creativity. He recommended that longitudinal (predictive) validation studies be initiated as quickly as possible. He also recommended Taylor's procedure of working first on the criterion Problem and then looking for the measures which should be used to predict them. One may refer to this process as post-current or follow-back validity in contrast to follow-up or predictive validity. Recommendations were also made concerning the desirability of cross-validation, the use of factor or sub-scores rather than just combinations of them, the need for using moderator variables (Carrying factors) and validation procedures other than the regression approach (such as comparing the mean scores of the successful scientists, with the means of the general population from which these scientists originally came). But very little empirical work seems to have come to print in this direction.

The most widely used tests for assessing creativity in children are the MTCT. However, do they measure what they purport to measure and to what extent do they predict later the creative ability.

Discussing this aspect Torrance (1962) comments that validity data of the usual kind is difficult to obtain in the case of creativity measures.

As such it is no wonder that different researchers used different procedures to establish validity of their tests. According to Treffinger, et al.,(1971) each instrument of creativity mirrored the particular set of beliefs and perceptions of its developer concerning the nature of creativity.

Torrance (1962) gives a variety of 'scattered evidence' for the validity of his tests. He found that his creativity tests discriminated industrial arts students rated as highly creative from those rated as least creative, saleswomen who sell most from those who sell least, and saleswomen who work in creative departments from those who work in routine departments. With elementary school children, it was validated in terms of observed behaviour in small groups situations, on the basis of achievement of the traditional kinds.

With regard to the question of prediction of later creative ability mentioned earlier, it was found in a 12 year follow up study of adolescents identified as creative in 1958 and 1959, that the youths identified as creative during high school tended to become productive adults. Young adults identified as highly creative in high school attained their peak creative achievement, in writing, medical and surgical discovery, dissertation research, musical composition, style of learning and human relations and organisation, more frequently compared to their less creative peers (Torrance, 1972).

Passi (1979) established concurrent validity of his creativity tests by correlating them with intelligence test scores, and achievement test scores.

Schaefer (1968) used teacher evaluation and creativity test scores as criterion measures to differentiate creative high school students in arts and science from a control group. To determine whether Barron-walsh Art scale is a good predictor of adolescent creativity, it was administered to the above two criterion groups. In general the creative achieved higher than the controls.

Schaefer (1969, 1972) also used teacher ratings and creativity test scores to establish the validity of the Biographical inventory of creativity.

While discovery the validity of his tests Misra (1986) observed 'we can say that the present tests of scientific creativity measures scientific creativity on the basis of (1) the way the tests have been developed and (2) the opinion expressed by nine experts'. He further validated his tests with teachers ratings and obtained rank correlations of 0.35 and 0.44 between teachers ratings and the creativity test scores.

Meholi (1973) correlated his creativity tests with teacher ratings. The correlations ranged between 0.32 and 0.40 for verbal tests and between 0.35 and 0.39 for non-verbal tests.

The following types of validity have been established for the battery of creativity tests used in the present study.

1. Construct or Concept Validity

The instrument in the present investigation was constructed in line with those of Torrance (1962), Getzels and Jackson (1962) and Wallach and Kogan (1965) giving due consideration to the relevance and familiarity of the items/objects to the average Indian children of the age group under investigation. The items were scrutinized by 6 judges who were conversant with creativity testing and suggestion given by them were incorporated before including them in the creativity tests designed for the investigation. Thus the test could reasonable be well assumed to have construct validity or concept validity in the words of cattell (1969).

2. Concurrent Validity

The scores on the instrument were correlated with those obtained on Raven's Progressive Matrices (RPM) to establish the concurrent validity of the instrument. Taylor and Barron (1964) summarily said 'most studies suggest that the relation of intelligence tests to creative performance is generally low (0.20 to 0.40) in unselected populations and is zero or even negative in homogeneous samples at higher levels of intelligence. Moss and Duenk (1967) reported correlations of 0.19 to 0.28 between both types of IQS and figural creativity, behavioural creativity and total creativity. Wodtke (1964) reported correlations of 0.23 to 0.54 between measures of intelligence and creativity. Torrance (1969a) reviewed 178 studies and obtained a median correlation of 0.20 between creativity and intelligence. According to Passi (1979) correlations between his test and RPM ranged between –0.01 and 0.81 for different sub-tests. The correlation between the creativity as measured by the whole test and verbal intelligence was 0.27, while it was 0.38 for non-verbal intelligence.

In the present case the creativity scores of 90 students selected by a stratified random sampling procedure, approximately evenly distributed between the two sexes, the two localities (urban and rural) and the three classes (VIII, IX and X) are correlated with their scores on the RPM.

The correlation coefficients thus obtained are presented in Table 4.1. It may be seen that in the case of verbal tests the correlation coefficients for fluency, flexibility, originality and total creativity scores were 0.42, 0.42, 0.41 and 0.53 respectively. In the case of non-verbal tests the correlation coefficient ranged between 0.38 and 0.46, while for the two types of tests put together the correlations varied between 0.40 and 0.50. The correlation coefficient for the different sub tests, each considered separately ranged between 0.16 and 0.89 in the case of verbal tests. It is needless to mention that these results are in line with those obtained by other investigators mentioned above.

Table 4.1: Correlation between creativity scores and scores on Ravens Progressive Matrices (N=90)

	Fluency	*Flexibility*	*Originality*	*Composite Creativity*
Verbal	0.42	0.42	0.41	0.53
Non-verbal	0.46	0.43	0.38	0.46
Verbal and Non-verbal put together	0.44	0.43	0.40	0.50

As pointed out earlier Taylor and Barron (1964) observed that in homogeneous samples at higher levels of intelligence, the correlation between creativity and intelligence would be zero or negative.

To probe into this the creativity scores of a homogeneous group of highly intelligent students was sought to be correlated with their intelligence scores.

Among the 90 students there were 22 who got a score of 40 or above on the RPM. The creativity scores of the 22 students were further analysed to see how they correlated with the scores on the RPM. The results obtained are shown in Table 4.2. It may be seen that all the correlation coefficients were negative.

Table 4.2: Correlation between creativity scores and scores on Ravens Progressive Matrices for a homogeneous group of highly intelligent students (N=22)

	Fluency	*Flexibility*	*Originality*	*Composite Creativity*
Verbal	−0.24	−0.30	−0.32	−0.17
Non-verbal	−0.15	−0.14	−0.14	−0.18
Verbal and Non-verbal put together	−0.26	−0.24	−0.30	−0.28

3. Criterion Validity

Several investigators like Schaefer (1968, 1969, 1972) Meholi (1973), Misra (1986) used teacher ratings as criteria for validating creative test scores. But the correlation coefficients between the two were not very high. Commenting on the low correlation Meholi (1973) remarked higher correlation with teacher ratings are usually not obtained due to the unreliability of the ratings.

Guilford (1954) observed that lack of clarity of the traits rated, and lack of adequate information on the part of the rater about the traits of the rates. Therefore the traits should be described properly and care should be taken to see that the raters know the raters fully well.

The most common errors in rating are leniency error of central tendency, halo effect etc,. These errors occur when the rater is asked to rate a large group of children. For example, when a teacher is rating 40 children he may not know well about all of them he may be tempted to be lenient and give higher rating to many or may tend to concentrate his rating around the mid point, avoiding ratings on either extreme. This effect will be minimised if the teacher is asked to nominate a few of those who are highest and a few who are least on a given trait. According to Nunnally (1959) teachers ratings of very good and very poor children are more valid. The errors can be further minimised if the meaning of the characteristic rated is properly understood by the rater (Champney, 1941).

Keeping this precautions in mind, in line with the procedure opted by Torrance (mentioned earlier) six teachers of VIII, IX, and X classes of a school were explained clearly the meaning of the concept of creativity and were, requested to nominate 5 most creative and 5 least creative students from each of their classes, on the basis of the type of their participation in different types of problem situations/activities in the class in particular, and in the school in general. The six groups of children were administered the creativity tests and their scores were analysed. The results obtained are shown in Table 4.3, 4.4 and 4.5.

Table 4.3: Means and SDS of the scores obtained on verbal tests by the high creative and low creative children as rated by the teachers and the results of *t* test.

	High creative	Low creative	
N	30	30	
M	525.15	420.57	5.43***
SD	85.21	62.14	

*** *t* Significant at 0.001 level.

Table 4.4: Means and SDS of the Scores obtained on Non-verbal tests by the high creative and low creative children as rated by the teachers and the results of the *t* test.

	High creative	Low creative	*t*
N	30	30	
M	164.27	115.21	7.60***
SD	37.59	22.11	

*** *t* Significant at 0.001 level.

Table 4.5: Means and SDs of the scores obtained on the entire test battery (Verbal and Non-verbal tests put together) by the high creative and low creative children as rated by the teachers and the results of *t* test.

	High creative	Low creative	*t*
N	30	30	
M	689.42	535.78	
SD	110.24	86.65	6.00***

*** *t* Significant at 0.001 level.

This shows that the creativity tests could discriminate between high creative and low creative children as judged by their teachers on the basis of the type of their participation in different types of problem situations and other activities. This was true for verbal tests, as well as non-verbal tests and also for all the tests put together.

Reliability

Reliability is especially important for evaluation of the creativity measures. Without information about the reliability of the creativity indices we would not know how to interpret whatever findings we obtain concerning the interrelationships, because the reliability of a measure after all functions as a ceiling or limit upon the extent to which it can reasonably be expected to relate to other variables (Wallach and Kogan, 1965).

Getzels and Jackson (1962) reported internal consistency reliability estimates for their creativity tests ranging between 0.81 and 0.87. The split half reliability of Wallach and Kogan tests varied between 0.51 and 0.93 for the different components on different sub-tests (Wallach and Kogan, 1965).

The split half reliability of Passi tests (Passi, 1979) of creativity ranged between 0.51 and 0.88. He reported the test-retest reliability for the different sub-tests ranging between 0.68 and 0.97. For the whole test battery the reliability co efficient was 0.92. Misra (1986) reported split half reliability of his tests to range between 0.50 and 0.63.

Torrance and Gowan (1963) found test-retest reliability for the MTCT to vary between 0.65 and 0.70 for the different sub-tests and 0.80 for the whole test. Hoepfner (1967) reported test-retest reliability for MTCT to range between 0.71 and 0.93. Moss and Duenk (1967) obtained reliability estimates rarying between 0.68 and 0.83 for this test, while Wodtke (1964) reported reliability coefficients between 0.28 and 0.75 for the verbal creativity test battery.

Mehdi (1973) reported test-retest reliability coefficients for his four verbal tests put together, ranging between 0.90 and 0.96. For the three non-verbal tests put together the reliability coefficients varied between 0.93 and 0.95 for different components of creativity.

The split half reliability coefficients of the battery of creativity tests used in the present investigation are presented in Table 4.6. It may be seen from the table that the reliability coefficient of verbal tests ranged between 0.78 and 0.83 for the different components of creativity. In the case of the non-verbal test the reliability coefficient varied between 0.79 and 0.82. The split half reliability for the different individual sub-tests was between 0.59 and 0.90 in the case of verbal tests, while it was between 0.75 and 0.90 in the case of non-verbal tests.

Table 4.6: Reliability coefficient of verbal, non-verbal, and the entire test battery (verbal and non-verbal tests put together N=90)

	Fluency	*Flexibility*	*Originality*	*Composite Creativity*
Verbal	0.78	0.80	0.83	0.80
Non-verbal	0.82	0.79	0.81	0.82
Verbal and Non-verbal put together	0.80	0.80	0.82	0.81

It may be seen that the reliability coefficient of the tests used in the present study are comparable to those obtained by other on investigators.

Measurement of Achievement Motivation

Achievement motivation has generally been measured by projective tests. Some efforts were made to develop some techniques for the measurement of achievement motivation in our country. Shomtamani and Hafeez (1968) developed a sentence completion test with three alternatives for measuring the achievement motivation of adult males. Aron *et al.*, (1969) developed a projective technique, consisting of five pictures for measuring the n-achievement of secondary school boys from South India. Mehtol (1969) adopted Mcclellands (1953) Thematic Apperception test technique for assessing the level of need achievement of high school students. Singh (1974) developed a short scale consisting of six items for measuring the achievement motivation of farmers. The Rao achievement motivation test has been developed to provide a simple and objective measure of achievement motivation of secondary school pupils.

There are 20 incomplete sentences each of which is followed by two possible alternatives A and B. Out of which one is an achievement motivated item. Though both the alternatives are achievement oriented and socially acceptable, yet one of them imply a higher sense of achievement and excellence.

Validity

The criterion validity coefficient of the Achievement Motivation Test as established by the author is 0.25.

Reliability

The reliability of the test was determined by the test-retest method, after an interval of one month. The coefficient of reliability was found to be 0.79.

Measurement of Scientific Attitude

Many writers have pointed out that knowledge about scientific facts and skill in the use of scientific methods are of little value if there is no inclination to use them. Scientific attitude represented the motivation which converts this knowledge and skill into action and refers to a willingness to use scientific procedures and methods.

It may best be described as 'an attitude towards ideas and information and particular ways of evaluating them', a formulation which distinguishes it from 'an attitude to science or scientists' on the one hand, and from' an ability to carry out scientific procedures' on the other (Gauld and Hukins, 1980).

Scientific attitude can be defined according to Noll (n.d) as having open mindedness, a desire for accurate knowledge, confidence in procedures for seeking knowledge and the expectation that the solution of the problem will come through the use of verified knowledge.

S.V. Scientific attitude scale was used in the present investigation to measure the scientific attitude of the children. It was developed by Venkata Rami Reddy in Telugu the regional language of Andhra Pradesh state. The items for the scale were collected from a number of sources like related literature, and from teachers of science and research students. The item pool thus prepared was gone through by judges drawn from the departments of Psychology and Education to check, edit, modifier and add other items, if necessary; their suggestions were incorporated and preliminary form of the scientific scale was prepared. The statements were arranged on a five point scale with five alternatives: strongly agree, agree, doubtful, disagree and strongly disagree, and such of those items that had a discriminative power significant at or above 0.05 level were selected to be included in the final form. The final form of the scientific attitude scale contains 40 items, 20 positive and 20 negative.

Validity

A. Content Validity

In the preparation of the instrument the items were collected from a number of sources as described earlier. The items were checked and rechecked by teachers of psychology and education to ascertain their relevance and coverage of the aspect under consideration. This establishes the content validity of the instrument.

B. Criterion Validity

At the end of the scientific attitude scale an item; I like to perform any activity only after analyzing it scientifically and critically; Yes/No; was given. Based upon their responses to the above item the subjects were categorised into two groups-A (those marking 'Yes') and B (those marking 'No'). The scientific attitude scores of the two groups were analysed applying *t* test. The results of the *t* test were presented in table.

It may be seen from the table the mean scores of those who marked 'Yes' to the above item was 151.74, while that of those who marked 'No' was 143.74. The *t* value for the difference between the two means was 2.45 which was significant at 0.05 level. Therefore, it may be concluded that the instrument has criterion validity.

Means and SDS of the scores obtained on the scientific attitude scale by group 'A' and group 'B' and the results of the *t* test

Group	*N*	*Mean*	*SD*	*t*
A	46	151.74	15.51	2.45*
B	54	143.74	16.87	

Note: *Significant at 0.01 level.

Reliability

The reliability of the scale was established by the split-half procedure. The reliability coefficient for the half test was 0.74. This was corrected by using Spearman-Brown prophecy formula, for the full length of the, test. The reliability coefficient thus obtained was 0.85 [N=100]

Measurement of 16 Personality Factors

The 16 PF Questionnaire developed by cattell *et. al* (1961) form C is used in the present study to measure personality variables. The have been established as unitary, psychologically meaningful entities in many researches in various life situations and enter into general psychological theory. These sixteen dimensions or scales are essentially independent. That is to say the correlation between one and another is usually negligible and having a certain position on one does not present the person's having any position whatever on another. Thus, each of the sixteen scales brings an entirely new piece of information about the person, a condition not found in many alleged multi dimensional scales. The 16 PF test comprehensiveness of personality coverage means that once obtained, its measurements can be used over and over again in different weightings, to predict any number of criteria.

Three alternative answers are provided for each of the 105 items, since the two alternative 'forced choice' situation, forbidding any 'middle of the road'. Compromise, tends to force an incorrect distribution of attitudes and often produces a version to the test on the part of the examine.

Validity

The validity of the test itself is meant to be an internal validity. That is to say, the items as stated above, are chosen as being good measures of the factors, as shown by factor analysis. The mean correlation of all single items with the factors they represent is +0.37, and the mean correlation of each group of six items with the factor it represents is about +0.71, which is decidedly high for so brief a test.

Reliability

Reliability has been worked out as test-retest correlation with a one-week interval between. The values obtained on a population of two hundred students. Some of these are not high, but their departure from unity, it must be remembered, covers function—fluctuation i.e., real changes in level of traits over times as well as just unreliability. Whenever higher reliability is more important than the increased demand on testing time, it can be raised by lengthening the rest, adding the 'A' and 'C' forms. Reliabilities will then range in the +0.75 to +0.95 area for each of the sixteen factors-scales.

Personal Data

Items such as Age, Sex, Education, Birth order, Locality, Family Literary Index, Father/Mother Occupation, Parent's Annual income are given at the front of the questionnaire to obtain the data related to personal, demographic variables included in the study.

SELECTION OF THE SAMPLE

The problem is aimed at measuring creativity of student teachers of DIETs. Students belonging to District Institute of Education and Training Institutes (DIETs) located in Rayalaseema Region** of Andhra Pradesh State, India.

The sample for the study was selected from the DIETs located in four districts [Chittoor, Cuddapah, Kurnool, Anantapur] which comprise Rayalaseema Region. 50 Male and 50 Female were selected at random from each of the institutes thus giving a total of '400' Ss for the study equally distributed between two sexes.

DIETs /Sex wise Distribution of the sample of Ss selected for the study

District	*Male*	*Female*	*Total*
Anantapur: DIET Bukkapatnam	50	50	100
Chittoor: DIET Karvetnagar	50	50	100
Cuddapah: DIET Rayachoti	50	50	100
Kurnool: DIET Kurnool	50	50	100
Total	**200**	**200**	**400**

ADMINISTRATION OF TOOLS

The subjects (Ss) were administered the instruments under normal class room conditions in small groups of not exceeding 20 at a time. The creativity tests were administered to the sample of Ss in a game like manner in line with Wallach and Kogan (1965), Venkatarami Raddy and Balakrishna Reddy (1983, 1984) without any time limit. Each of the 10 sub-tests of the creativity test battery were administered separately.

The Ss were seated comfortably and they were told about the nature and importance of the investigation so as to motivate them to take the tests in a right spirit. Before administering each sub test, the students were explained what they had to do, with the help of the example given in the instructions to each sub-test.

The creativity tests were administered in the morning session of the college, giving a gap of 15 minutes after the first 7 sub-tests. Achievement motivation, scientific attitude and 16 personality factor (Form-C) scale were administered giving a gap of 10 minutes after completion of each test. All these instruments were administered as per the instructions given in the respective manuals which were explained in Telugu, the regional language of the subjects.

The total time taken for administration of all the tests put together was about three and a half hours including the time taken for instructions etc.

SCORING

Creativity (Verbal, Non-verbal and Composite Creativity)

Much care has to be exercised in scoring the responses for the items in creativity tests, as there are no right or wrong responses. To enhance the objectivity of scoring the usual procedure adopted is to get the responses scored by different scores and to see that the inter scorer reliability is high.

The responses of the Ss were scored based upon the following procedure suggested by Guilford (1951) Torrance (1962) and Child (1973) and followed by various investigators like Gakhar (1974) Badrinath and Satyanarayanan (1979)

Venkatrami Reddy and Balakrishna Reddy (1983, 1984) Chandra and Ghose (1985) Misra (1986) Syama Thirumurthi (1987) Venkatrami Reddy and Vijaya Kumari (1989) Venkatrami Reddy and Sudhakar Reddy (1990) Sivarathnam Reddy (1994) Raja Sekhar Reddy (1997) etc.

(i) Fluency

A fluency score was obtained by totalling the number of relevant responses given by the subjects. Responses that were non-sensical or which did not answer the question as posed, were eliminated before counting the responses.

(ii) Flexibility

A flexibility score was obtained by categorizing the responses into as many discrete qualifications as suggest themselves. Clearly, the subjectivity of the scorer comes into any measure of flexibility so derived, but consensus agreement among a number of scores was employed by was of making the final flexibility score more objective.

(iii) Originality

Different procedures were suggested by different authors to determine the originality. In the present investigation in line with Guilford (1952) and Torrance (1962) originality was defined in terms of the statistical infrequency of a given response in a given population. Since originality as defined by statistical infrequency of a response is only relative, each response is original in its own right, though the degree of originality of different responses. Many vary depending upon the statistical infrequency of each of them, Guilford (1952) discriminated 5 levels of uncommonness, each level representing one fifth of the total responses. Andrews (1930) also rated originality on a 5 point scale on the basis of a frequency tally of the responses of the students in the group. Thus a response given by 20 per cent or less number of subjects of the sample was given an originality score of 5, while response given by 21% to 40% of the Ss was given a score of 4, similarly responses given by 41% to 60%, 61% to 80% and 81% and above were given originality scores of 3,2 and 1 respectively.

(iv) Composite Creativity Scores

The scores of the subjects on the 3 components of creativity [Fluency, Flexibility and Originality] were added to give a total verbal and non-verbal creativity score for each subject, following Torrance (1962). However, the composite scores are obtained by adding verbal and non-verbal creativity scores.

Achievement Motivation

The achievement motivation test was scored by assigning numerical values to the two sets of responses. Each item of the test is followed by two responses of which one is high achievement related (HAR) and the other is general achievement at a higher level were assigned a score of three where as the general achievment related statements depicting achievement at a lower level were assigned a score of one. The maximum and minimum scores on the test would be 60 and 20.

Scientific Attitude

Scientific attitude statements were arranged on a five point scale with five alternatives. The final form of the scientific attitude scale contains 40 items, 20 positive and 20 negative.

Sixteen Personality Factors

16PF questionnaire was scored as per the weights provided by the authors. Except the items in factor-B all the other items were placed on a 3 point scale with weights, 0, 1, 2 for the items in factor-B the weights are 0 and 1.

Scoring Weightages of Personal Data Sheet

The information provided by the respondents in the personal data sheet was also numerically coded to suit the computer analysis.

ANALYSIS OF THE DATA

The total scores obtained by each of 400 subjects all the 26 variables were computed. The data were carefully analysed by employing appropriate statistical techniques.

To estimate the general level of creativity of student teachers of DIETs all the descriptive, statistics such as mean, median, mode, range, Q.D, S.D, Sknewness and Kurtosis were calculated. To study the influence of independent variables on creativity inferential statistics such as 't' test and 'F' test were employed. Finally step wise regression analysis was carried out to identify the contribution made by each one of the independent variables to creativity of student teachers of DIETs.

The detailed analysis of the data and the discussions made on the results are presented in the succeeding chapter.

REFERENCES

1. Telugu is the regional language of the people, of Andhra Pradesh where this investigation was conducted.
2. The creativity test battery is presented in Appendix A Its English version is presented in Appendix B_1.

5

Results and Discussion

This chapter has been presented in 4 sections. The first section describes the distribution of scores obtained by the subjects on the dependent variables. All the descriptive statistics of these distributions are calculated and discussed. In the second section the influence of personal and demographic variables on the dependent variables are studied. Section three throws light on the influence of psychological variables on dependent variables. In the fourth section the prediction of dependent variables has been made with the help of different independent variables.

DISTRIBUTION OF SCORES

The creativity, as explained earlier, was measured by using verbal and non-verbal test and a composite creativity score was also obtained for all subjects. The scores of these variables—verbal, non-verbal and composite—are presented in the form of distributions to study the system of distributions with the help of different descriptive statistics.

Description of Distribution of Verbal Creativity Scores

The dependent variable in the study is creativity. As explained earlier the total verbal creativity scores for each individual is calculated and presented in the form of a frequency distribution table. All the descriptive statistics are calculated and necessary discussions are made to see, whether the distribution follows normality.

The verbal creativity scores spread from 299 to 1211. The range is 912.000. The mean creativity score 606.690 indicates that

Table 5.1: Frequency Distribution of Verbal Creativity Scores

C.I.	*Mid Point*	*Frequency*	*Smoothed Frequency*	*Cumulative Frequency*
250-350	300	6	19.33	6
351-450	400	52	50.33	58
451-550	500	93	87.66	151
551-650	600	118	94.33	269
651-750	700	72	72.33	341
751-850	800	27	39.33	368
851-950	900	19	17.33	387
951-1050	1000	6	10.33	393
1051-1150	1100	5	4.33	398
1151-1250	1200	2	2.33	400
		400		

Mean	: 606.690		QD	: 85.500
Median	: 589.000		SD	: 156.393
Mode	: 553.620		SK	: 0.895
Range	: 912.000		KU	: 4.535

Fig.1: The Distribution of Verbal Creativity Scores
a. Frequency Polygon

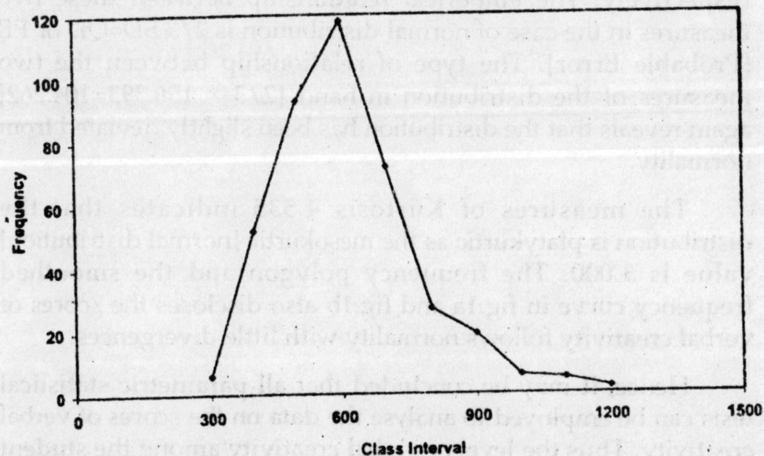

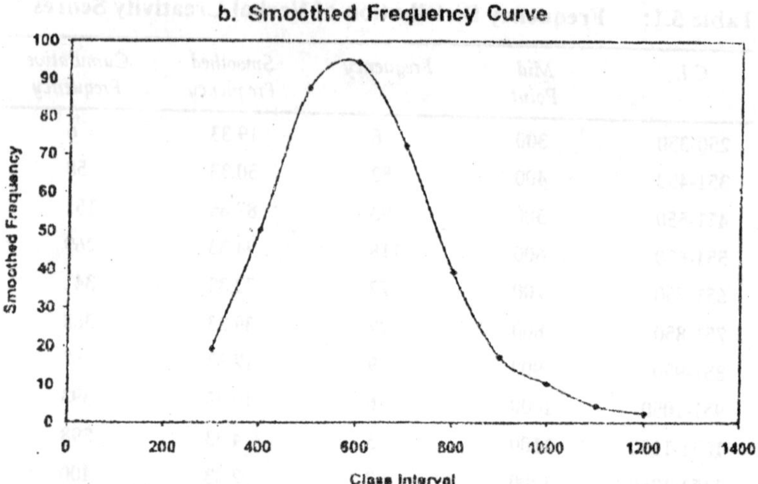

majority of the subjects have been scored above the mid-point. The general level of creativity is slightly greater than the average point. The median and mode values are 589.000 and 553.620 respectively. As the measures of central tendency values are in the descending order it can be said that the distribution has been positively skewed. The calculated value of skewness i.e., 0.895 also confirms that the distribution has been skewed positively.

The measures of dispersion both Quartile Deviation [QD] and Standard Deviation [SD] values are 85.500 and 156.393 respectively. The emperical relationship between these two measures in the case of normal distribution is 2/3 SD=QD or PE [Probable Error]. The type of relationship between the two measures of the distribution in hand [2/3 × 156.393=104.262] again reveals that the distribution has been slightly deviated from normality.

The measures of Kurtosis 4.535 indicates that the distribution is platykurtic as the mesokurtic [normal distribution] value is 3.000. The frequency polygon and the smoothed frequency curve in fig.1a and fig.1b also discloses the scores of verbal creativity follows normality with little divergences.

Hence, it may be concluded that all parametric statistical tests can be employed to analyse the data on the scores of verbal creativity. Thus the level of verbal creativity among the student teachers of DIETs is more than the mid-point of the creativity scale and hence, it can be concluded that the existing level of verbal creativity among the student teachers of DIETs is above average level.

Description of Distribution of Non-verbal Creativity Scores

The dependent variable in the study is creativity. As explained earlier the Non-verbal total creativity for each individual was calculated and presented in the form of frequency distribution. All the descriptive statistics are calculated and necessary discussions are made to see whether the distribution follow any normality.

Table 5.2: Frequency Distribution of Non-verbal Creativity Scores

C.I.	*Mid Point*	*Frequency*	*Smoothed Frequency*	*Cumulative Frequency*
150-200	175	16	23.33	16
201-250	225	54	56.33	70
251-300	275	99	87.00	169
301-350	325	108	95.00	277
351-400	375	78	72.00	355
401-450	425	30	39.66	385
451-500	475	11	14.66	396
501-550	525	3	5.00	399
551-600	575	1	1.33	400
		400		

Mean	: 316.247	Q.D	: 47.500
Median	: 312.000	S.D	: 71.320
Mode	: 303.505	SK	: 0.169
Range	: 433.000	KU	: 3.2491

The Non-verbal creativity scores spread from 151 to 584. The range is 433.000. The mean creativity scores 316.247 indicates majority of the subjects are scored above the mid-point. The general level of creativity is greater than the average point. The median value and mode value are 312.000 and 303.505

Fig.2: The Distribution of Non-verbal Creativity Scores
a. Frequency Polygon

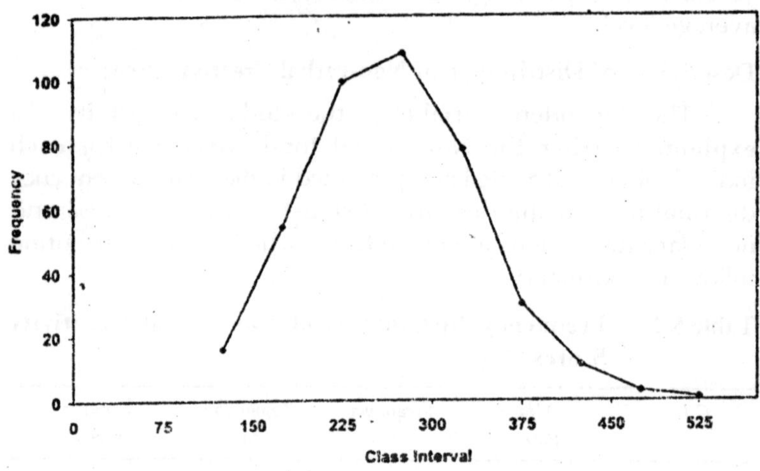

b. Smoothed Frequency Curve

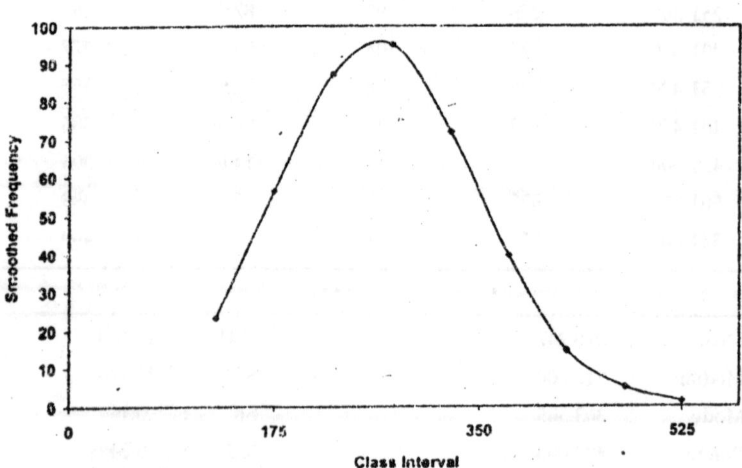

respectively. As the measures of central tendency values are in the descending order it can be said that the distribution of scores has slight positive skewness. The calculated value of skewness is 0.169 also confirms that the distribution is positively skewed to the little extent.

The measures of dispersion both Quartile Deviation [QD] and Standard Deviation [SD] values are 47.500 and 71.320 respectively. The empirical relationship between these two measures in the case of normal distribution is 2/3 SD=QD or PE [Probable Error]. This type of relationship between the two measures of the distribution in hand [2/3 × 71.320=47.546] reveals that the distribution is almost normal.

The measures of Kurtosis 3.249 indicates the distribution is mesokurtic. The frequency polygon and the smoothed frequency curve in fig 2a and fig 2b also discloses the scores of Non-verbal creativity follows normality with very little divergences.

Hence, it may be concluded that all parametric statistical tests can be employed to analyse the data on the scores of non-verbal creativity. Thus the level of Non-verbal creativity among the student teachers of DIETs is more than the midpoint on the creativity scale and hence, it can be concluded that existing level of non-verbal creativity among the student teachers of DIETs is above average.

Description of Distribution of Composite Creativity Scores

The dependent variable in the study is creativity. As explained earlier, the composite index of creativity [verbal+non-verbal components] for each individual was calculated and presented in the form of a frequency distribution. All the descriptive statistics were calculated and necessary discussions were made to see whether the distribution follows normality.

The composite index of creativity scores, spread from 426 to 1662. The range is 1236.000. The mean creativity score 921.192 indicates that majority of the subjects are scores above the mid-point. The general level of creativity is slightly greater than the average point. The median and mode values are 916.000 and 905.615 respectively. As the measures of central tendency values are in the descending order it can be said that the distribution of scores has slight positive skewness. The calculated value of skewness is 0.297. It also confirms that the distribution is positively skewed to the little extent.

Table 5.3: Frequency Distribution of Composite Creativity Scores

C.I.	*Mid Point*	*Frequency*	*Smoothed Frequency*	*Cumulative Frequency*
401-500	450	1	7.33	1
501-600	550	21	16.66	22
601-700	650	28	35.00	50
701-800	750	56	56.00	106
801-900	850	84	74.00	190
901-1000	950	82	78.33	272
1001-1100	1050	69	59.33	341
1101-1200	1150	27	37.66	368
1201-1300	1250	17	16.66	385
1301-1400	1350	6	8.66	391
1401-1500	1450	3	4.33	394
1501-1600	1550	4	3.00	398
1601-1700	1650	2	2.00	400
		400		

Mean	: 921.192		SK	: 0.297
Median	: 916.000		KU	: 3.949
Mode	: 905.615		Q.D	: 120.000
Range	: 1236.000		S.D	: 196.591

The measures of dispersion both Quartile Deviation [QD] and Standard Deviation [SD] values are 120.000 and 196.591 respectively. The empirical relationship between these two measures in the case of normal distribution is 2/3 SD=QD or PE Probable Error]. This type of relationship between the two measures of the distribution in hand [2/3 × 196.591=131.060] again reveals that the distribution is slightly deviating from normality.

The measure of kurtosis 3.949 indicates that the distribution is platykurtic as the mesokurtic [normal distribution] value is 3.000. The frequency polygon and the smoothed frequency curved in fig. 3a and fig. 3b also revealed that the distribution is normal with little divergences.

Fig 3: The Distribution of Composite Creativity Scores

a. Frequency Polygon

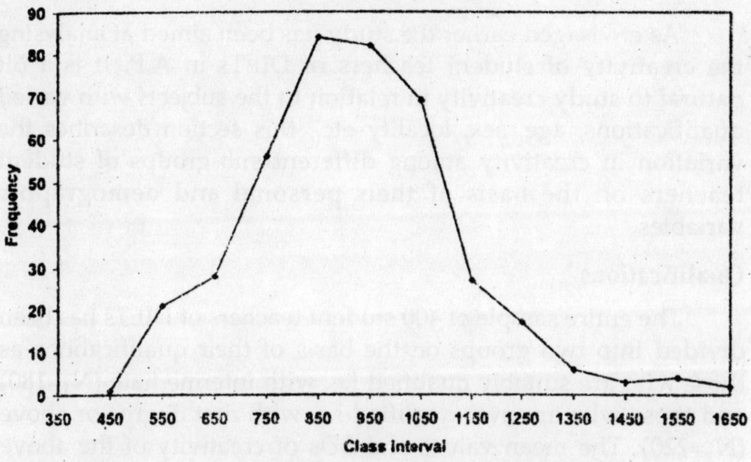

b. Smoothed Frequency Curve

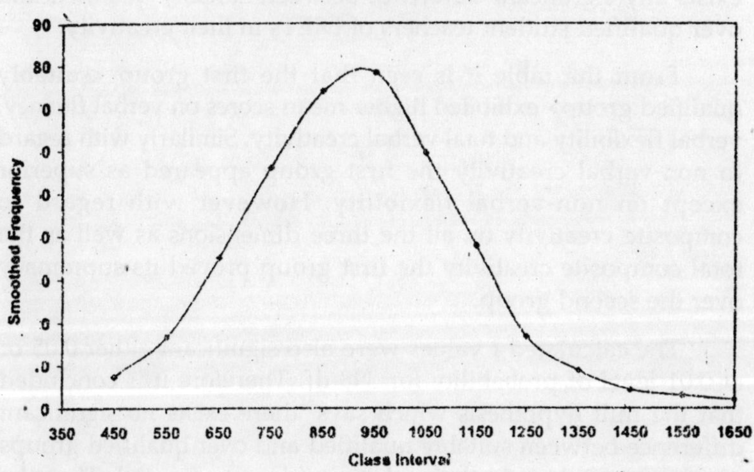

Hence, it may be concluded that all Parametric statistical tests can be employed to analyse the data on the scores of creativity. Thus the level of creativity among the student teachers of DIETs' is more than the mid-point on the creativity scale and hence, it can be concluded that the existing level of creativity among the student teachers of DIETs is above average level.

THE INFLUENCE OF PERSONAL AND DEMOGRAPHIC VARIABLES ON CREATIVITY

As envisaged earlier the study has been aimed at analysing the creativity of student teachers of DIETs in A.P. It is a bit natural to study creativity in relation to the subjects with varied qualifications, age, sex, locality etc., this section describes the variation in creativity among different sub-groups of student teachers on the basis of their personal and demographic variables.

Qualifications

The entire sample of 400 student teachers of DIETs has been divided into two groups on the basis of their qualifications as those who are suitably qualified i.e. with intermediate (N_1=180) and those who are over-qualified i.e. with first degree or above (N_2=220). The mean values and SDs of creativity of the above two sub-samples are presented in table 5.4 to see whether there exists any significant difference between suitably qualified and over qualified student teachers of DIETs in their creativity.

From the table it is seen that the first group <suitably qualified group> exhibited higher mean scores on verbal fluency, verbal flexibility and total verbal creativity. Similarly with regard to non-verbal creativity the first group appeared as superior except on non-verbal flexibility. However with regard to composite creativity on all the three dimensions as well as the total composite creativity the first group proved its supremacy over the second group.

The calculated *t* values were also significant either 0.05 or at 0.01 level of probability for 398 df. Therefore it is concluded that the null hypothesis which says 'there exists no significant difference between suitably qualified and over qualified groups of student teachers in their creativity' is not accepted. Thus the student teachers, with suitable qualifications are more creative than the over qualified student teachers of DIETs.

Age

With regard to age the sample of 400 student teachers of DIETs has divided into three groups on the basis of their age i.e.,

Table 5.4: Means and SD's of Creativity Scores of Student Teachers of DIETs Whose Qualifications are (Intermediate; N_1-180; Degree and above: N_2-220)

	N	*M*	*SD*	*t*
Verbal Fluency	180	107.500	28.215	2.426*
	220	100.818	26.720	
Verbal Flexibility	180	45.522	4.860	2.068*
	220	44.568	4.355	
Verbal Originality	180	471.183	136.457	1.901@
	220	446.972	118.110	
Total Verbal Creativity	180	624.205	165.774	2.301*
	220	592.359	147.488	
Non-verbal Fluency	180	49.305	11.636	3.443**
	220	45.509	10.395	
Non-verbal Flexibility	180	32.383	5.295	1.828*
	220	31.454	4.846	
Non-verbal Originality	180	246.000	58.549	2.855**
	220	229.922	53.860	
Total Non-verbal Creativity	180	327.688	74.042	2.925**
	220	306.886	67.924	
Composite Fluency	180	156.805	34.083	3.134**
	220	146.327	32.541	
Composite Flexibility	180	77.905	8.003	2.225*
	220	76.022	7.342	
Composite Originality	180	717.183	167.069	2.236*
	220	676.894	151.005	
Total Composite Creativity	180	951.893	203.926	2.431*
	220	899.245	188.590	

1. up to 20 yrs [N_1=160]
2. 21-23 yrs [N_2=166]
3. 24 and above yrs [N_3=74]

The mean creativity scores of these three groups of students teachers of DIETs were analysed to see whether their age could influence their creativity significantly. The mean scores and SD's of the three groups were presented in the following table.

From the table it can be observed that the appropriate age group of (younger age group) student teachers of DIETs exhibit higher mean scores on the three dimensions of verbal creativity and non-verbal creativity (fluency, flexibility, originality). Consequently with regard to the three dimensions of composite creativity fluency, flexibility, originality–as well as the total creativity the appropriate age group of student teachers of DIETs proved its supremacy. Thus the younger age group of student teachers are more creative than the other age groups.

The calculated *F* values were also significant at 0.01 level of probability for 2,397 df. Therefore, the null hypothesis 'that there exists no significant difference among appropriate age group (younger age group) and the two older age groups of student teachers of DIETs in their creativity' is not accepted.Thus the appropriate age group of student teachers are more creative than the older age group of student teachers of DIETs.

The above findings coincides with the results of Raina (1970) Khire (1970) Passi (1972) Lalithamma (1973) Joshi (1974) Badrinath & Satyanarayana (1979) Dharmagandan (1981) Venkatrami Reddy & Balakrishna Reddy (1984) Vewnkateswara Rao (1987) Venkatrami Reddy & Saleena (1988).

Sex

The total sample of 400 student teachers of DIETs was divided into two groups on the basis of their sex of the subjects. The mean scores of male and Female student teachers and the corresponding standard deviations were presented in the table to see whether there exists any significant difference between male and female groups of student teachers in their verbal creativity, non-verbal creativity and composite creativity.

Table 5.5: Means and SDs of Creativity Scores of Student Teachers of DIETs on the Basis of Age (20 years; N_1-160; 21-23 years; N_2-166; 24 and above; N_3-74)

	N	M	SD	t
Verbal Fluency	160 166 74	112.025 100.524 93.500	29.248 25.363 23.600	14.357**
Verbal Flexibility	160 166 74	46.162 44.602 43.364	5.066 3.952 4.332	10.882**
Verbal Originality	160 166 74	493.356 442.084 416.540	141.050 112.529 106.260	12.061**
Total Verbal Creativity	160 166 74	651.543 587.210 553.405	171.498 139.705 133.016	12.853**
Non-verbal Fluency	160 166 74	49.643 45.891 44.945	11.419 11.115 9.504	6.720**
Non-verbal Flexibility	160 166 74	32.618 31.542 31.000	5.265 4.775 5.120	3.218**
Non-verbal Originality	160 166 74	247.468 231.885 226.689	57.500 50.752 48.081	4.742**
Total Non-verbal Creativity	160 166 74	329.731 309.319 302.635	72.459 72.575 61.928	5.080**
Composite Fluency	160 166 74	161.668 146.415 138.445	34.516 31.635 29.251	16.032**
Composite Flexibility	160 166 74	78.780 76.144 74.364	7.748 7.109 7.958	9.292**
Composite Originality	160 166 74	740.824 673.969 643.229	170.388 147.508 136.417	11.432**
Total Composite Creativity	160 166 74	981.274 896.529 856.040	207.151 183.616 171.820	12.531**

Table 5.6: Means and SDs of Creativity Scores on the Basis of Sex (Male; N_1-200; and Female; N^2-200) Student Teachers of DIETs and the *t* Values

	N	*M*	*SD*	*t*
Verbal Fluency	200	89.480	20.147	12.176**
	200	118.170	26.541	
Verbal Flexibility	200	43.300	3.911	7.916**
	200	46.695	4.635	
Verbal Originality	200	396.550	90.726	11.005**
	200	519.185	128.857	
Total Verbal Creativity	200	529.330	112.875	11.354**
	200	684.050	156.182	
Non-verbal Fluency	200	42.000	9.130	10.617**
	200	52.435	10.479	
Non-verbal Flexibility	200	29.865	5.122	8.618**
	200	33.880	4.142	
Non-verbal Originality	200	210.175	44.999	10.857**
	200	264.140	54.002	
Total Non-verbal Creativity	200	282.040	58.357	10.905**
	200	350.455	66.831	
Composite Fluency	200	131.480	25.886	14.199**
	200	170.605	28.865	
Composite Flexibility	200	73.165	7.553	11.122**
	200	80.575	5.768	
Composite Originality	200	606.725	117.854	13.020**
	200	783.325	147.507	
Total Composite Creativity	200	811.370	148.963	13.489**
	200	1034.505	176.409	

The table reveals that the Female student teachers of DIETs exhibited higher mean scores on the three dimensions of verbal creativity <fluency, flexibility, originality> Similarly with regard to non-verbal creativity the female student teachers appeared as superior. Consequently with regard to composite creativity on all the three dimensions as well as on the total composite creativity the female student teachers of DIETs proved their supremacy over the male student teachers of DIETs.

The calculated *t* values were also significant at 0.01 level of probability for 398 df. Therefore, the null hypothesis that 'there exists no significant difference between male and female student teachers of DIETs in their creativity' is not accepted. Thus the female student teachers are more creative than the male student teachers of DIETs. The finding reported is similar to the reports of Getzels and Jacksons (1962) Raina (1970) Passi (1972) Hussain (1974) Singh (1975) Pandit (1976) Brodley (1976) Rawat and Garg (1977) Jurial (1981) Chadha (1981) Pandey(1984) Chanda and Ghose (1985) Rajasekhar Reddy (1997).

Birth Order

With regard to birth order the sample of 400 student teachers of DIETs was divided into three groups on the basis of their birth order. (1) 1st born [N_1=156] (2) 2nd born [N_2=109] (3) later born [N_3=135]. The creativity scores of these three groups of student teachers were analysed to see whether the birth order could influence the creativity significantly. The mean scores and standard deviations of the three groups were presented in the following table.

It can be observed from the above table that the mean scores of creativity of the three groups of student teachers first born, second born, and later born are more or less same on all the dimensions of creativity (fluency, flexibility, originality) and on total creativity whether it is measured verbally or non-verbally. Consequently the results of composite creativity also reveal slight or marginal variations without indicating any tend leading to guess any significant influence of birth order on creativity.

The obtained *F* value could not reach the table value even at 0.05 level of probability for 2,397 df. Therefore, the null

Table 5.7: Means and SDs of Creativity Scores Student Teachers of DIETs on the Basis of Birth Order (Ist Born; N_1-156; IInd Born N_2-109; IIIrd Born and above; N_3-135) and *F* Values

	N	*M*	*SD*	*F*
Verbal Fluency	156 109 135	102.955 105.972 103.096	26.357 28.745 28.080	0.454@
Verbal Flexibility	156 109 135	45.006 45.440 44.629	4.339 4.479 4.998	0.932@
Verbal Originality	156 109 135	451.833 468.559 456.207	118.121 139.870 126.732	0.571@
Total Verbal Creativity	156 109 135	599.794 619.972 603.933	146.623 169.262 157.626	0.563@
Non-verbal Fluency	156 109 135	46.737 47.220 47.770	11.048 10.882 11.441	0.311@
Non-verbal Flexibility	156 109 135	31.673 31.761 32.192	5.231 4.795 5.111	0.414@
Non-verbal Originality	156 109 135	232.916 239.908 239.837	55.573 56.260 57.910	0.719@
Total Non-verbal Creativity	156 109 135	311.326 318.889 319.800	70.518 70.293 73.502	0.610@
Composite Fluency	156 109 135	149.692 153.192 150.866	32.625 34.827 33.884	0.390@
Composite Flexibility	156 109 135	76.679 77.201 76.821	7.860 7.708 7.510	0.073@
Composite Originality	156 109 135	684.749 708.467 696.044	145.872 176.973 159.334	0.650@
Total Composite Creativity	156 109 135	911.120 938.861 923.733	183.967 212.328 198.874	0.572@

hypothesis that 'there exists no significant influence of birth order on creativity of student teachers of DIETs' is accepted. It is concluded that birth order has no significant influence on the creativity of student teachers of DIETs.

The results reported are similar to the report of Datta (1968) Srivastava (1977) Badrinadh and Satyanarayana (1979) Kaur (1986) Harmek and Manjit (1988) Venkatrami Reddy and Tulsi Devi (1988).

Locality

The entire sample of 400 student teachers of DIETs are from both rural and urban localities viz. <rural N_1=270 and urban N_2=130>. The mean scores of student teachers belonging to rural and urban localities and the respective standard deviations along with the *t* values have been depicted in the following table.

From the table it is seen that the urban student teachers exhibited higher mean scores on the three dimensions of verbal creativity <fluency, flexibility, originality> consequently with regard to the total verbal creativity the urban student teachers appeared as superior. On non-verbal fluency, flexibility and originality as well as on the total non-verbal creativity the urban student teachers proved their supremacy over the rural student teachers. Consequently, the results show the same pattern in composite creativity too.

However the calculated *t* values were also significant either 0.05 or at 0.01 level of probability for 398 df. except on non-verbal fluency and flexibility. Therefore the null hypothesis that 'there exists no significant difference between rural and urban student teachers in their creativity' is not accepted. Thus it is concluded that the urban student teachers are more creative than the rural. The results reported is similar to the reports of Passi (1971) Singh (1977) Singh (1978) Srivastava (1978) Dharmagandan (1981).

Family Literacy Index

On the basis of education status of all the members in the family, a Family Literacy Index has been developed by employing a simple, average method—total number of years of education obtained by each member in the family divided by

Table5.8: Means and SDs of Creativity Scores of Rural (N_1-270; and Urban; N_2-130) Student Teachers of DIETs and the *t* Values

	N	*M*	*SD*	*t*
Verbal Fluency	270	101.770	25.087	2.158*
	130	108.092	31.802	
Verbal Flexibility	270	44.66	4.595	2.078*
	130	45.684	4.576	
Verbal Originality	270	448.115	114.467	2.213*
	130	478.038	148.459	
Total Verbal Creativity	270	594.592	141.819	2.237*
	130	631.815	181.542	
Non-verbal Fluency	270	46.470	10.440	2.943*
	130	48.769	12.310	
Non-verbal Flexibility	270	31.577	5.041	2.679*
	130	32.484	5.087	
Non-verbal Originality	270	232.203	51.529	2.543**
	130	247.466	64.692	
Total Non-verbal Creativity	270	310.251	65.828	2.435*
	130	328.700	80.648	
Composite Fluency	270	148.240	30.701	2.332*
	130	156.861	38.487	
Composite Flexibility	270	76.243	7.689	2.623*
	130	78.168	7.500	
Composite Originality	270	680.358	140.630	2.602*
	130	725.484	189.376	
Total Composite Creativity	270	904.843	176.613	2.606*
	130	960.515	229.743	

total number of persons in the family. Basing on the literacy index the sample of 400 student teachers is divided into three groups.

1. Low Literacy 0-5 <N_1=108>

   Moderate Literacy 6-10 <N_2:176>

   High Literacy 11 and above <N_3:116>

The mean creativity scores and SDs of the three groups of student teachers of DIETs have been shown in the following table.

From the table 5.8 it is seen that the low Family Literacy Index group of student teachers exhibited low mean scores on the three dimensions of verbal creativity <Fluency, Flexibility, Originality> similarly with regard to non-verbal creativity, the low Family Literacy Index group of student teachers appeared as inferior. However with regard to composite creativity on all the three dimensions as well as on the total creativity the low Family Literacy Index Group of student teachers of DIETs proved their low level of creativity when compared to the moderate and High Literacy Index groups of student teachers of DIETs.

The calculated *F* values were also significant at 0.01 level of probability for 2,397 df. Therefore, the null hypothesis that 'there exists no significant influence of student teachers family literacy index on their creativity' is not accepted. Thus, it is concluded that the family literacy index has a significant bearing on the creativity of the student teachers. In other words lower the family literacy index low was the creativity, of course after a particular level. Whether the family literacy index was moderate or high, there was no much difference in the creativity of student teachers of DIETs.

Occupation

The sample of 400 student teachers of DIETs was divided into three groups on the basis of the occupation of their father viz (1) Labour [N_1: 107] (2) Agriculture, [N_2: 155] (3) Secured job [N_3: 138]. The table of mean creativity scores and standard deviations of three groups were as follows in table 5.9.

An observation in to the table the labour occupation group of student teachers exhibited low mean scores on the three

Table 5.9: Means and SDs of Creativity Scores on the Basis of Family Literacy Index (Low; 0-5: N_1-108; Moderate 6-10: N_2-176; High 11 and above; N_3-116) Student Teachers of DIETs and the *F* Values

	N	*M*	*SD*	*F*
Verbal Fluency	108	92.231	24.029	13.930**
	176	108.045	25.533	
	116	108.215	30.576	
Verbal Flexibility	108	43.240	4.148	11.619**
	176	45.483	4.366	
	116	45.896	4.957	
Verbal Originality	108	406.092	105.980	13.020**
	176	–477.732	118.032	
	116	475.931	114.750	
Total Verbal Creativity	108	541.564	132.060	13.606**
	176	631.261	145.742	
	116	630.043	176.256	
Non-verbal Fluency	108	42.629	9.726	13.406**
	176	48.789	11.142	
	116	49.103	11.175	
Non-verbal Flexibility	108	29.666	4.806	15.021**
	176	32.636	5.004	
	116	32.676	4.824	
Non-verbal Originality	108	213.101	47.210	14.471**
	176	244.562	56.757	
	116	248.319	57.912	
Total Non-verbal Creativity	108	285.398	60.785	14.897**
	176	325.988	71.345	
	116	330.189	72.619	
Composite Fluency	108	134.860	29.398	18.167**
	176	156.834	30.875	
	116	157.318	36.549	
Composite Flexibility	108	72.906	7.211	19.666**
	176	78.119	7.092	
	116	78.663	7.841	
Composite Originality	108	619.193	129.790	17.322**
	176	722.294	144.345	
	116	724.250	183.090	
Total Composite Creativity	108	826.962	164.007	18.271*
	176	957.249	179.807	
	116	960.232	221.066	

Table 5.10: Means and SDs of Creativity Scores of Student Teachers of DIETs on the Basis of Occupation of the Father (Labour; N_1-107; Agriculture; N_2-155; Secured Job; N_3-138)

	N	*M*	*SD*	*F*
Verbal Fluency	107 155 138	95.299 103.961 110.282	23.976 27.220 28.934	9.273**
Verbal Flexibility	107 155 138	43.336 45.496 45.724	3.865 4.914 4.491	10.012**
Verbal Originality	107 155 138	421.336 458.825 485.115	102.882 129.338 135.158	7.856**
Total Verbal Creativity	107 155 138	559.972 608.283 641.123	128.627 158.923 165.283	8.407**
Non-verbal Fluency	107 155 138	45.056 47.283 48.818	9.400 12.244 10.813	3.498**
Non-verbal Flexibility	107 155 138	30.588 31.658 33.108	4.631 5.277 4.901	7.942**
Non-verbal Originality	107 155 138	224.486 236.606 247.826	46.621 60.329 57.353	5.272**
Total Non-verbal Creativity	107 155 138	300.130 315.348 329.753	59.710 76.686 71.376	5.318**
Composite Fluency	107 155 138	140.355 151.244 159.100	28.545 34.070 34.710	9.470**
Composite Flexibility	107 155 138	73.924 77.154 78.832	6.605 8.058 7.440	12.565**
Composite Originality	107 155 138	645.822 695.431 732.941	125.971 159.755 172.440	8.799**
Total Composite Creativity	107 155 138	860.102 923.631 970.876	158.746 199.615 208.446	9.398**

dimensions of verbal creativity (fluency, flexibility, originality). Similarly with regard to non-verbal creativity the labour occupation group of student teachers appeared as inferior. Consequently with regard to composite creativity on all the three dimensions as well as on the total creativity the labour occupation group of student teachers of DIETs proved their low level of creativity when compared to the Agriculture and secured job occupation groups of student teachers of DIETs.

The *F* ratios obtained are greater than the table value for 2,397 df at 0.01 level of probability. Therefore, the null hypothesis that 'there exists no significant influence of student teachers occupation on the creativity' is accepted. It is concluded that the occupation of the father has a significant bearing on the creativity of the student teachers. Secured job group of student teachers are more creative than the other counterparts.

In the past two decades studies on creativity in relation to father's occuption has not been reported.

Annual Income

With regard to Annual Income, the sample of 400 student teachers of DIETs was divided into three groups on the basis of their family Annual Income i.e., (1) 1-10 thousands [N_1: 138] (2) 11-50 thousands [N_2: 135] (3) 51 thousands and above [N_3: 127]. The scores of the three groups of student teachers of DIETs were analysed to see whether the Annual Income could experience their creativity significantly. The mean scores and standard deviations of the three groups were presented in the following table.

The table indicates that the high income group student teachers exhibited higher mean scores on the three dimensions of verbal creativity (fluency, flexibility, originality). Similarly with regard to non-verbal creativity the high income group student teachers appeared as superior except on non-verbal fluency. Consequently with regard to composite creativity fluency, flexibility, originality as well as the total creativity the high income group student teachers proved their supremacy.

The *F* ratios obtained are greater value than the table value of 2,397 df at 0.05 level of probability. Therefore, the null

Table 5.11: Means and SDs of Creativity Scores of Annual Income Groups (1-10 Thousands: N_1-138; 11-50 Thousands: N_2-135; 51 Thousands and above: N_3-127) Students Teachers of DIETs

	N	*M*	*SD*	*F*
	138	100.710	23.006	
Verbal Fluency	135	103.192	29.772	2.306[@]
	127	107.881	29.345	
	138	44.304	3.981	
Verbal Flexibility	135	45.318	5.227	2.412[@]
	127	45.409	4.488	
	138	442.260	99.870	
Verbal Originality	135	459.503	140.075	1.971[@]
	127	473.086	137.643	
	138	587.275	124.586	
Total Verbal Creativity	135	608.014	172.684	2.080[@]
	127	626.377	168.080	
	138	46.043	9.678	
Non-verbal Fluency	135	47.274	12.206	1.533[@]
	127	48.433	11.322	
	138	31.347	4.5621	
Non-verbal Flexibility	135	31.577	5.771	2.924[@]
	127	32.755	4.701	
	138	229.405	49.216	
Non-verbal Originality	135	237.888	60.795	2.489[@]
	127	244.803	58.528	
	138	306.797	62.542	
Total Non-verbal Creativity	135	316.740	77.414	2.411[@]
	127	325.992	72.990	
	138	146.753	27.544	
Composite Fluency	135	150.466	37.192	2.705[@]
	127	156.314	35.113	
	138	75.651	6.651	
Composite Flexibility	135	76.895	8.925	3.672[*]
	127	78.164	7.125	
	138	671.665	122.592	
Composite Originality	135	697.391	174.714	2.437[@]
	127	717.889	174.657	
	138	894.072	154.204	
Total Composite Creativity	135	924.754	218.448	2.607[@]
	127	952.369	210.941	

hypothesis that 'there exists no significant influence of Annual income on creativity of student teachers of DIETs is accepted. Thus, it is concluded that the Annual income has no significant influence on the creativity. The high income group student teachers are more creative than the other group student teachers of DIETs.

THE INFLUENCE OF PSYCHOLOGICAL VARIABLES

As described in Chapter III, Achievement Motivation, Scientific attitude and Personality factors are measured and '$M \pm \frac{1}{2}\sigma$' or 1st and 3rd quartile points were used to divide the sample into 3 groups as high, moderate and low groups in the respective variable. The creativity scores of these groups are analysed to see whether there exists any significant influence of these psychological variables on creativity.

Influence of Achievement Motivation

The entire sample of 400 student teachers of DIETs was divided into three groups on the basis of their Achievement motivation scores i.e., low <N_1=129>, moderate <N_2=163> and high <N_3=108>. The mean values and SDs of Creativity of the above show whether there exists any significant difference between groups in their creativity.

It is found from the table that the mean creativity scores of the three groups appears to be more or less the same on the three dimensions of verbal creativity <fluency, flexibility, originality>. Similarly with regard to non-verbal creativity the student teachers appears more or less the same. Hence, with regard to composite creativity as well as the total composite creativity the student teachers mean scores are more or less the same.

The calculated *F* values did not reach the table value even at 0.05 level for 2,397 df. Hence, it is concluded that the null hypothesis 'there exists no significant difference among low, moderate and high achievement motivation groups of student teachers in their creativity' is accpeted.

Influence of Scientific Attitude

With regard to Scientific attitude, the sample for 400 student teachers of DIETs was divided into three groups on the basis of their scientific attitude i.e., (i) low [N_1: 136] (ii) moderate

Table 5.12: Means and SDs of Creativity Scores of Student Teachers of DIETs whose Achievement Motivation Scores are (low: N_1-129; Moderate: N_2-163; High: N_3-108)

	N	*M*	*SD*	*F*
Verbal Fluency	129 163 108	101.108 104.368 106.250	29.565 27.268 25.448	1.075@
Verbal Flexibility	129 163 108	44.620 44.895 45.601	4.638 4.716 4.383	1.403@
Verbal Originality	129 163 108	441.480 463.061 469.601	135.387 125.924 117.500	1.673@
Total Verbal Creativity	129 163 108	587.209 612.325 621.453	165.980 155.495 145.411	1.588@
Non-verbal Fluency	129 163 108	47.953 47.619 45.731	12.319 10.724 10.110	1.355@
Non-verbal Flexibility	129 163 108	32.077 32.104 31.277	5.614 4.964 4.500	1.019@
Non-verbal Originality	129 163 108	242.209 237.748 230.231	62.780 53.522 52.722	1.337@
Total Non-verbal Creativity	129 163 108	322.240 317.472 307.240	79.292 68.080 65.949	1.339@
Composite Fluency	129 163 108	149.06 151.987 151.981	37.754 32.137 30.608	0.309@
Composite Flexibility	129 163 108	76.697 76.999 76.878	8.940 6.827 7.344	0.073@
Composite Originality	129 163 108	683.689 700.809 699.832	183.074 146.774 146.676	0.662@
Total Composite Creativity	129 163 108	909.450 929.797 928.693	223.936 183.548 181.829	0.577@

Table 5.13: Means and SDs of Creativity Scores of Students Teachers of DIETs whose Scientific Attitude Scores are (low: N_1-136; Moderate: N_2-151; High: N_3-113)

	N	*M*	*SD*	*F*
Verbal Fluency	136 151 113	105.169 105.549 99.902	29.902 29.546 22.584	1.605[@]
Verbal Flexibility	136 151 113	45.080 45.451 44.283	4.445 5.260 3.735	2.141[@]
Verbal Originality	136 151 113	459.948 465.463 445.212	136.323 132.138 107.359	0.847[@]
Total Verbal Creativity	136 151 113	610.198 616.470 589.398	166.121 164.851 131.326	1.017[@]
Non-verbal Fluency	136 151 113	47.816 47.516 46.097	12.046 10.917 10.202	0.824[@]
Non-verbal Flexibility	136 151 113	32.213 31.973 31.327	5.464 4.971 4.685	0.990[@]
Non-verbal Originality	136 151 113	239.779 239.059 231.460	61.036 55.169 52.600	0.805[@]
Total Non-verbal Creativity	136 151 113	319.808 318.549 308.884	77.312 69.784 66.048	0.947[@]
Composite Fluency	136 151 113	152.985 153.065 145.999	35.901 35.192 27.849	1.806[@]
Composite Flexibility	136 151 113	77.293 77.430 75.610	8.002 7.711 7.159	2.188[@]
Composite Originality	136 151 113	699.727 704.522 676.672	174.493 160.723 136.255	1.007[@]
Total Composite Creativity	136 151 113	930.006 935.019 898.289	213.001 201.624 167.611	1.161[@]

[N_2: 151] (iii) high [N_3: 113]. The mean scores of these three groups of student teachers of DIETs were analysed to see whether the scientific attitude could influence the creativity significantly.

From the table it is seen that the mean creativity scores of the three groups appears to be more or less the same on the three dimensions of verbal creativity except on verbal flexibility. Similarly with regard to non-verbal creativity the student teachers mean scores appears more or less the same. Therefore with regard to creativity as well as the total creativity the student teachers mean scores are more or less the same.

The calculated *F* values did not reach the table value even at 0.05 level of probability for 2.397 df, except in the cases of verbal flexibility and composite flexibility. Hence, it is concluded that the null hypothesis that 'there exists no significant difference between low and high scientific attitude groups of student teachers in their creativity' is accepted.

Influence of Personality Factors in Creativity

The 16 primary source factors measured by the 16 personality factor questionnaire, were considered to study the personality of student teacher of DIETs. To identify the influence of these factors one by one on the creativity of student teachers of DIETs. The sample of subjects was divided into three groups on the basis of their scores on each one of the 16 personality factors.

Low group : Those who scored upto the first quartile on respective personality factor.

Moderate group : Those who scored in between the first and the third quartile on each one of the personality factor.

High group : Those who scored above third quartile on the respective personality factor.

The range of the scores on each factor in each quartile varies. The creativity scores of these criterion groups were analysed to study the influence of each one of the personality factors on their creativity.

CREATIVITY-FACTOR—A

Table 5.14: Means and SDs of Creativity Scores of Student Teachers of DIETs with Different Levels on Factor. A of 16 PF (LOW: N_1-147; Moderate: N_2-125; High: N_3-128)

	N	*M*	*SD*	*F*
Verbal Fluency	147 125 128	103.265 106.736 101.625	28.090 29.014 25.403	1.135@
Verbal Flexibility	147 125 128	45.102 44.936 44.937	4.965 4.561 4.247	0.586@
Verbal Originality	147 125 128	456.020 471.744 446.437	131.520 137.177 110.335	1.279@
Total Verbal Creativity	147 125 128	604.387 623.416 593.000	160.907 168.345 138.309	1.219@
Non-verbal Fluency	147 125 128	47.394 46.464 47.750	11.786 10.108 11.317	0.450@
Non-verbal Flexibility	147 125 128	31.646 31.824 32.179	5.455 4.895 4.787	0.385@
Non-verbal Originality	147 125 128	238.061 235.200 238.031	61.327 51.978 55.393	1.108@
Total Non-verbal Creativity	147 125 128	317.102 313.488 317.960	77.180 65.757 70.281	0.140@
Composite Fluency	147 125 128	150.659 153.200 149.375	34.591 35.103 31.025	0.426@
Composite Flexibility	147 125 128	76.748 76.760 77.116	7.927 8.036 7.057	0.456@
Composite Originality	147 125 128	694.081 706.944 684.738	172.287 162.338 139.946	0.526@
Total Composite Creativity	147 125 128	921.489 936.904 910.960	209.238 202.754 175.982	0.468@

The student teachers who scored low on the continuam of Factor 'A' tend to be stiff, cool, aloof. They work alone and avoid clash with others view point. They are likely to be precise, rigid in their doing things and in personal standards. They tend to be times critical abstractive or hard.

Who scored high on the factor 'A' tend to be good nature, easy going, ready to cooperate, soft hearted, kind trustful and adoptable. They are generous in personal relation less afraid of criticism but oftenless dependable in precision work and in obligation.

An observation into the mean values depicted in table reveals that there is no clear trend either in verbal, non-verbal and composite creativity (fluency, flexibility, originality) on some dimensions the middle group of factor A scored high creative scores and on some the high group scored high, but these differences appeared to be only due to sampling fluctuations and not because of the variations in factor 'A'.

The calculated *F* ratios in all the situations also revealed that these differences are not statistically significant as the obtained *F* ratios are far below the table values even at 0.05 level of probability for 2,397 df. Therefore the null hypothesis that 'there exists no significant influence of factor A of 16 PF on creativity of student teachers of DIETs' is accepted. Thus it could be concluded that personality factor of the factor A of 16 PF could not significantly influence the level of creativity among the student teachers of DIETs.

Cattell and Butcher (1968) prepared a profile of personality factors for the creative person on the basis of studies on several samples of adults. It has been found by them that creatives score lower than the mean for the general population on this factor. The results of the present study collaborate the findings of Cattell and Butcher.

The person scoring low on factor 'B' tends to be slow general ability slow to learn and grasp, dull, sluggish. High on factor 'B' tends to be quick to grasp ideas, a fast learner, intelligent. The above table reveals that the factor B of 16PF about the individuals trait of dull and bright a fast learner, intelligent. There is a clear trend either in verbal, non-verbal and composite

CREATIVITY-FACTOR—B

Table 5.15: Means and SDs of Creativity Scores of Student Teachers of DIETs with Different Levels on Factor—B of 16 PF (Low: N_1-159; Moderate: N_2-145; High: N_3-96)

	N	*M*	*SD*	*F*
Verbal Fluency	159 145 96	104.666 103.634 102.718	25.724 28.526 29.254	0.154@
Verbal Flexibility	159 145 96	45.169 44.875 44.895	4.525 4.653 4.713	0.184@
Verbal Originality	159 145 96	463.440 454.137 454.270	118.063 128.611 139.691	0.252@
Total Verbal Creativity	159 145 96	613.276 602.648 601.885	145.785 158.854 171.069	0.233@
Non-verbal Fluency	159 145 96	48.981 46.993 44.635	11.261 11.336 10.076	4.703**
Non-verbal Flexibility	159 145 96	32.471 32.082 30.562	5.001 5..286 4.638	4.521**
Non-verbal Originality	159 145 96	246.069 236.469 223.437	56.918 57.835 51.321	4.910**
Total Non-verbal Creativity	159 145 96	327.522 315.544 298.635	71.959 73.001 64.808	5.007**
Composite Fluency	159 145 96	153.647 150.627 147.354	31.546 35.041 34.685	1.048@
Composite Flexibility	159 145 96	77.640 76.957 75.457	7.135 8.179 7.692	2.247@
Composite Originality	159 145 96	709.509 690.606 677.707	149.467 166.447 162.779	1.565@
Total Composite Creativity	159 145 96	940.798 918.192 900.520	185.273 204.234 202.897	1.0529@

creativity three dimensions the low personality group on factor B scored high creative scores.

The *F* ratios obtained in all the situations also reveals that these differences are not statistically significant as the obtained *F* ratios are far below the table values even at 0.05 level of probability for 2,397 df. In verbal creativity, originality and composite creativity. Therefore the null hypotheses that 'there exists no significant influence of Factor 'B' of 16 PF on creativity of student teachers of DIETs' is not accepted in non-verbal creativity. Thus it is concluded that the personality factor 'B' of 16 PF has significant influence on the level of creativity among the student teachers of DIETs. Therefore the student teachers with the traits of low general ability Vs intelligence (or) Dull Vs bright differ significantly in their non-verbal creativity.

Factor 'B' on the 16 PF is related to general intelligence. It has been found by many as reported in the previous chapter, that there is a significant relationship between creativity and intelligence. Though high intelligence does not guarantee high creativity. It is no wonder therefore that the low creative group student teachers exhibited a higher level of intelligence than the high creative group.

As mentioned earlier (Chapter II) even those who contend that creativity and intelligence are independent, agree that certain amount of intelligence is essential for any creative work. Only after a minimum level of intelligence is reached intelligence and creativity get separated (Mackinnon,1962, Taylor, 1964, Vernon, 1964, Barron, .1969, Sharma, 1974, Rawat and Agarwal, 1977, Quereshi, 1982, Venkatarama Reddy and Balakrishna Reddy, 1983, Ashok, 1985).

The person who scores low on factor 'C' tends to be emotionally immature, lacking in frustration tolerance, worrying easily annoyed, generally dissatisfied, having neurotic symptoms. High on factor 'C' tends to be emotionally mature, stable, calm, phlegmatic, realistic about life, placid, possessing ego strength, having an integrated philosophy of life. It can be observed from the above table that the mean scores of creativity of the three groups of student teachers are more or less same on all the three dimensions of creativity. Whether it is measured verbally, non-verbally and composite creativity on factor 'c' of 16PF.

CREATIVITY-FACTOR--C

Table 5.16: Means and SDs of Creativity Scores of Student Teachers of DIETs with Different Levels on Factor. C of 16PF (low: N_1-110; Moderate: N_2-211; High: N_3-79)

	N	*M*	*SD*	*F*
	110	103.463	29.785	
Verbal Fluency	211	103.962	26.552	0.013@
	79	103.962	27.385	
	110	44.709	5.269	
Verbal Flexibility	211	45.066	4.333	0.325@
	79	45.215	4.369	
	110	456.627	141.530	
Verbal Originality	211	458.052	120.231	0.009@
	79	459.101	125.416	
	110	604.800	171.944	
Total Verbal Creativity	211	607.080	149.336	0.012@
	79	608.278	155.046	
	110	46.063	11.246	
Non-verbal Fluency	211	47.028	10.467	2.058@
	79	49.329	12.418	
	110	31.481	5.136	
Non-verbal Flexibility	211	31.772	4.539	1.381@
	79	32.683	6.175	
	110	234.409	58.316	
Non-verbal Originality	211	234.895	52.140	1.507@
	79	247.025	64.383	
	110	311.954	72.806	
Total Non-verbal Creativity	211	313.696	66.152	1.605@
	79	329.038	81.769	
	110	149.526	36.315	
Composite Fluency	211	150.990	31.818	0.317@
	79	153.291	34.648	
	110	76.190	8.019	
Composite Flexibility	211	76.838	6.986	1.984@
	79	77.898	8.820	
	110	691.036	180.282	
Composite Originality	211	692.947	144.923	0.331@
	79	706.126	165.849	
	110	916.754	217.278	
Total Composite Creativity	211	920.776	181.815	0.373@
	79	937.316	207.003	

CREATIVITY-FACTOR—E

Table 5.17: Means and SDs of Creativity Scores of Students Teachers of DIETs with Different Levels on Factor. E of 16PF. (LOW: N_1-152; Moderate: N_2-130; High: N_3-118)

	N	*M*	*SD*	*F*
Verbal Fluency	152 130 118	107.947 100.500 102.178	29.595 25.714 26.372	2.882[@]
Verbal Flexibility	152 130 118	45.486 44.400 45.025	5.099 4.303 4.211	1.960[@]
Verbal Originality	152 130 118	483.960 435.769 448.601	141.993 111.172 118.043	5.607[**]
Total Verbal Creativity	152 130 118	637.394 580.669 595.805	173.987 137.267 147.239	5.104[**]
Non-verbal Fluency	152 130 118	48.171 45.938 47.398	12.460 10.811 9.452	1.437[@]
Non-verbal Flexibility	152 130 118	31.947 31.630 32.042	5.689 4.837 4.463	0.229[@]
Non-verbal Originality	152 130 118	242.453 229.576 238.686	64.84 52.757 47.960	1.888[@]
Total Non-verbal Creativity	152 130 118	322.572 307.146 318.127	81.556 67.179 60.681	1.698[@]
Composite Fluency	152 130 118	156.118 146.438 149.576	36.455 31.592 31.256	3.121[*]
Composite Flexibility	152 130 118	77.433 76.030 77.067	8.599 7.346 6.753	0.826[@]
Composite Originality	152 130 118	726.413 665.345 687.287	177.693 142.525 144.250	5.777[**]
Total Composite Creativity	152 130 118	959.966 887.815 913.932	220.324 174.648 180.275	5.163[**]

The obtained *F* value could not reach the table value even at 0.05 level of probability for 2,397 df. Therefore the null hypothesis that 'there exists no significant influence of factor 'c' of 16PF on creativity of student teachers of DIETs' is accepted. Thus it is concluded that the factor 'c' of 16PF could not significantly influence the level of Creativity among the student teachers of DIETs.

According to Cattell this factor is the core of frustration tolerance. There is no gain saying emotional maturity, calm and unruffled nature, and more than anything else, perserverance and frustration tolerance are essential for creative thinking. Neurotic tendency indeed, hampers rather than helps creativity.

Cattell and Butcher (1968) found from their studies on a number of samples of creative individuals that high creatives scored for higher on this factor than the average.

The factor 'E' of 16PF speaks about the individuals trait of submissive Vs dominant. An observation into the mean values depicted in table reveals that there is a clear trend either in verbal, non-verbal creativity and composite creativity the low personality group were proved to be more creative. The student teachers who scored low tend to be humble, accommodating, expressive and soft-hearted were more creative than the high scores who tend to be tough minded, hard and authoritarian.

The calculated *F* values were also significant at 0.01 level of probability for 2,397 df. Therefore, the null hypothesis that 'there exists no significant influence of factor 'E' of 16PF on creativity of student teachers of DIETs' is not accepted. Thus it is concluded that the personality factor E of 16PF has significant influence the level of creativity of student teachers of DIETs. Therefore the student teachers with the traits of submissive Vs Dominant differ significantly in their creativity. However, the differences in the creativity of three groups were not significant in the case of non-verbal creativity although there was trend in-favour of submissive group.

Cattell (1969) points out that 'high dominance may lead to disobedience, head strong self will, independence and creativity of mind, and sometimes antisocial behaviour. But the more direct expressions are often controlled, and in sublimated from the trait

CREATIVITY-FACTOR—F

Table 5.18: Means and SDs of Creativity Scores of Student Teachers of DIETs with Different Levels on Factor. F of 16PF. (LOW: N_1-141; Moderate: N_2-136; High: N_3-123)

	N	*M*	*SD*	*F*
Verbal Fluency	141 136 123	103.212 105.375 102.813	28.531 27.266 26.923	0.331@
Verbal Flexibility	141 136 123	44.879 45.441 44.642	4.845 4.705 4.200	1.042@
Verbal Originality	141 136 123	458.035 465.250 449.512	129.049 125.250 127.422	0.493@
Total Verbal Creativity	141 136 123	606.127 616.066 596.967	159.955 155.201 154.866	0.480@
Non-verbal Fluency	141 136 123	47.687 47.536 46.325	11.854 11.283 10.052	0.576@
Non-verbal Flexibility	141 136 123	32.000 32.000 31.585	5.479 5.260 4.336	0.283@
Non-verbal Originality	141 136 123	238.581 238.330 234.227	58.194 57.823 53.370	0.238@
Total Non-verbal Creativity	141 136 123	318.269 317.867 312.138	74.352 72.908 66.532	0.293@
Composite Fluency	141 136 123	150.899 152.911 149.138	35.607 33.324 31.678	0.382@
Composite Flexibility	141 136 123	76.879 77.431 76.227	8.104 7.761 7.083	0.960@
Composite Originality	141 136 123	696.616 703.580 683.739	164.525 154.456 158.670	0.667@
Total Composite Creativity	141 136 123	924.396 933.933 909.105	205.761 193.352 190.670	0.637@

is not always rated undesirable. For example good sports performance and independence and creativity in arts and sciences are associated with dominance.

From the results of the present study, however creativity seems to be associated with submissiveness rather than dominance.

The Student teachers who scored low tend to be sober, introspective, reticent and who scored high were impulsive, mercurial, and talkative. It can be observed from the above table that the mean scores of creativity of the three groups of student teachers are more or less the same on all the three dimensions of creativity. Whether it is measured verbally or non-verbally, consequently the results of composite creativity also reveals slight or marginal variations without indicating any trend leading to guess any significant influence of factor 'F' of 16PF.

The obtained *F* values could not reach the table value even at 0.05 level of probability for 2,397 df. Therefore the null hypothesis that 'there exists no significant influence of Factor F of 16PF on creativity' of student teachers of DIETs' is accepted. It is concluded that the factor 'F' of 16PF has no bearing on the creativity of student teachers of DIETs.

A look into the table revealed that the high group of student teachers were proved to be more creative when compared to other two groups. The student teachers who have achieved more on factor 'G' were considered as conscientious, preserving rule bound i.e., stronger super ego strength (G^+) were proved to be more creative than the student teachers of weak super ego strength (G^-).

The factor G of 16 personality factor speaks about the individuals trait of casual Vs conscientious. It is evident from the table the high group student teachers of DIETs on this factor of personality exhibited higher mean scores on the three dimensions of verbal and non-verbal creativity. However with regard to composite creativity the high group student teachers exhibited higher mean scores of creativity.

The calculated *F* values were also significant at 0.01 level of probability for 2,397 df. Therefore the null hypothesis that

CREATIVITY-FACTOR—G

Table 5.19: Means and SDs of Creativity Scores of Student Teachers of DIETs with Different Levels on Factor-G of 16PF, (Low: N_1-145; Moderate: N_2-124; High: N_3-131)

	N	*M*	*SD*	*F*
Verbal Fluency	145 124 131	104.744 97.814 108.496	25.842 26.407 29.596	5.006**
Verbal Flexibility	145 124 131	44.786 44.459 45.740	4.561 4.737 4.473	2.722@
Verbal Originality	145 124 131	458.420 430.338 483.313	122.595 115.665 137.494	5.664**
Total Verbal Creativity	145 124 131	607.951 572.612 637.549	149.247 144.617 169.488	5.611**
Non-verbal Fluency	145 124 131	48.944 45.121 47.290	11.298 9.497 12.049	4.016**
Non-verbal Flexibility	145 124 131	32.489 31.153 31.870	4.537 5.087 5.533	2.338@
Non-verbal Originality	145 124 131	245.896 225.064 238.931	56.404 47.792 62.385	4.723**
Non-verbal Creativity	145 124 131	327.331 301.338 318.091	70.841 61.258 78.670	4.573**
Composite Fluency	145 124 131	153.688 142.935 155.786	31.923 31.838 35.832	5.597**
Composite Flexibility	145 124 131	77.275 75.612 77.610	7.112 7.685 8.148	3.242**
Composite Originality	145 124 131	704.316 655.402 722.244	154.743 142.796 172.393	5.982**
Total Composite Creativity	145 124 131	935.282 873.950 955.640	187.968 180.066 213.600	5.976**

CREATIVITY-FACTOR—H

Table 5.20: Means and SDs of Creativity Scores of Student Teachers of DIETs with Different Levels on Factor-H of 16 PF, (Low N_1-151; Moderate: N_2-132; High: N_3-117)

	N	*M*	*SD*	*F*
Verbal Fluency	151 132 117	102.218 104.560 105.068	29.150 27.372 25.768	0.421@
Verbal Flexibility	151 132 117	44.834 45.371 44.786	4.861 4.599 4.284	0.649@
Verbal Originality	151 132 117	454.178 457.689 462.829	137.225 128.342 112.144	0.152@
Total Verbal Creativity	151 132 117	601.231 607.621 612.683	169.285 156.086 140.334	0.179@
Non-verbal Fluency	151 132 117	47.814 47.545 46.076	11.242 11.354 10.693	0.890@
Non-verbal Flexibility	151 132 117	31.980 32.265 31.290	5.543 5.140 4.271	1.201@
Non-verbal Originality	151 132 117	240.264 239.113 230.940	57.337 57.465 54.321	1.015@
Total Non-verbal Creativity	151 132 117	320.059 318.924 308.307	72.826 72.411 68.334	1.031@
Composite Fluency	151 132 117	150.032 152.105 151.144	36.303 32.680 31.187	0.126@
Composite Flexibility	151 132 117	76.814 77.636 76.076	8.565 7.029 7.161	1.131@
Composite originality	151 132 117	694.442 696.802 693.769	170.613 162.629 140.335	0.002@
Total Composite Creativity	151 132 117	921.290 926.545 920.990	213.432 195.826 176.200	0.013@

'there exists no significant influence of factor 'G' of 16PF on creativity among the student teachers of DIETs' is not accepted. It is concluded that the factor 'G' of 16 PF has significant influence on creativity among the student teachers of DIETs.

A number of studies indicate that the score on this factor determines 'success in a variety of performances requiring persistance, freedom from oscillation and good organisation of thinking. Cattell (1969), Joshi (1974) also found that high creatives had a higher super ego strength.

A Person who scores high on the factor tends to be adventurous, sociable, participating, ready to try newthings, spontaneous, which are likely to make him more creativity prone, compared to qualities like shy, withdrawing, retiring, cool, restricted interests, which are characteristics of low scorers on this factor.

An observation into the mean values depicted in table reveals that there is no clear tend either in verbal or non-verbal creativity. All the three groups on factor 'H' scored more or less the same. Consequently the results show the same pattern in composite creativity too.

The calculated *F* values were also did not reach the table value even at 0.05 level of probability for 2,397 df. Therefore the null hypothesis that 'there exists no significant influence of Factor 'H' of 16 PF on creativity of student teachers of DIETs' is accepted. It is concluded that the factor H of 16PF has no impact on the creativity of student teachers of DIETs.

It has been found that on I+ individual (one who scores, high on the factor I) shows a definite dislike for crude people and rough occupations. He has a taste for romantic travel and new experiences. He is imaginative and has an aesthetic mind and a love of dramatics. Artists score high on this factor (Cattell, 1969) this shows that an I+ prone to be more creative.

An observation into the mean values depicted in table reveals that there is no clear trend either in verbal or non-verbal creativity. Consequently the results show the same pattern in composite creativity too.

CREATIVITY-FACTOR—I

Table 5.21: Means and SDs of Creativity Scores of Student Teachers of DIETs with Different Levels on Factor-I of 16 PF, (Low: N_1-136; Moderate: N_2-146; High: N_3-118)

	N	*M*	*SD*	*F*
Verbal Fluency	136 146 118	102.911 105.876 102.339	30.435 28.013 23.286	0.649@
Verbal Flexibility	136 146 118	44.970 44.952 45.084	4.982 4.742 3.986	0.032@
Verbal Originality	136 146 118	460.316 436.561 448.000	144.808 129.112 100.475	0.526@
Total Verbal Creativity	136 146 118	608.198 614.390 595.423	177.749 158.451 125.871	0.486@
Non-verbal Fluency	136 146 118	46.294 48.016 47.237	12.119 10.927 10.114	0.889@
Non-verbal Flexibility	136 146 118	31.073 32.411 32.127	5.567 4.854 4.630	2.684@
Non-verbal Originality	136 146 118	234.816 240.500 235.720	61.579 57.025 49.653	0.408@
Total Non-verbal Creativity	136 146 118	312.193 320.972 315.084	77.828 71.359 63.573	0.554@
Composite Fluency	136 146 118	149.205 153.892 149.576	37.447 33.739 28.427	0.792@
Composite Flexibility	136 146 118	76.043 77.363 77.211	7.790 8.030 7.069	1.457@
Composite Originality	136 146 118	695.132 704.061 683.720	181.842 162.260 124.641	0.322@
Total Composite Creativity	136 146 118	920.381 935.362 910.507	224.709 198.469 157.546	0.344@

The calculated *F* ratios in all the situations also reveals that these differences are not statistically significant as the obtained *F* ratios are far below the table values even at 0.05 level of probability for 2,397 df. Therefore the null hypothesis that 'there exists no significant influence of Factor I to 16 PF on creativity of student teachers of DIETs' is accepted. Thus it can be safely concluded that the Factor I to 16PF was not associating with the level of creativity.

The Student teachers who scored low on factor-L tend to be free of jealous tendencies, cheerful, concerned about other people, a good team worker whereas high scores are considered as self opinionated, competitive and interested in internal mental life.

An observation into the mean values depicted in table, explains that there is a clear trend either in verbal or in non-verbal creativity the lower group on Factor 'L' Scored high creative scores consequently the results show the same pattern in composite creativity too.

The calculated *F* values were also significant either at 0.05 or at 0.01 level of probability for 2,397 df. Therefore the null hypothesis that 'there exists no significant influence of factor *L* of 16PF on creativity of student teachers of DIETs' is not accepted. Thus, it can be concluded that the factor L of 16 PF has significant influence on the level of creativity among the student teachers of DIETs.

The person who scores low on factor 'M' is considered to be as anxious to do the right thing, practical and conformist. Where as high scorers are tend to be unconventional, unconcerned, egocentric, sensitive, imaginative. It could be seen from the above table there is no much deviations in mean scores whether in verbal or in non-verbal creativity. Consequently in composite creativity scores also the differences were not found too divergent.

The calculated *F* ratios could not reach the table value even at 0.05 level of probability for 2,397 df. Therefore the null hypothesis that 'there exists no significant influence of factor 'M' of 16PF on creativity of student teachers of DIETs' is accepted.

CREATIVITY-FACTOR—L

Table 5.22: Means and SDs of Creativity Scores of Student Teachers of DIETs with Different Levels on Factor-L of 16 PF, (Low: N_2-106; Moderate: N_2-145; High: N_3-149)

	N	*M*	*SD*	*F*
Verbal Fluency	106 145 149	109.245 104.317 99.489	29.495 28.049 25.024	3.972^{*}
Verbal Flexibility	106 145 149	45.707 44.855 44.630	5.125 4.401 4.387	$1.805^{@}$
Verbal Originality	106 145 149	488.990 458.013 435.583	139.639 130.583 109.256	5.593^{**}
Total Verbal Creativity	106 145 149	643.943 607.186 579.704	171.448 159.509 136.993	5.326^{**}
Non-verbal Fluency	106 145 149	48.952 47.427 45.778	10.730 11.837 10.535	$2.584^{@}$
Non-verbal Flexibility	106 145 149	32.566 31.951 31.302	5.492 5.306 4.445	$1.962^{@}$
Non-verbal Originality	106 145 149	245.943 239.331 228.791	55.759 62.410 49.856	3.051^{*}
Total Non-verbal Creativity	106 145 149	327.462 318.710 305.872	70.326 78.177 63.936	$2.995^{@}$
Composite Fluency	106 145 149	158.197 151.744 145.267	35.055 34.235 31.006	4.790^{**}
Composite Flexibility	106 145 149	78.273 76.806 75.932	7.899 7.820 7.317	$2.378^{@}$
Composite Originality	106 145 149	734.933 697.344 664.374	167.603 168.385 137.540	5.721^{**}
Total Composite Creativity	106 145 149	971.405 925.896 885.576	207.925 204.613 173.707	5.612^{**}

CREATIVITY-FACTOR—M

Table 5.23: Means and SDs of Creativity Scores of Student Teachers of DIETs with Different Levels on Factor-M of 16 PF. (Low: N_1-109; Moderate: N_2: 158; High: N_3-133)

	N	*M*	*SD*	*F*
Verbal Fluency	109 158 133	106.137 103.113 102.774	26.598 30.254 24.978	0.531@
Verbal Flexibility	109 158 133	45.220 45.227 44.541	4.483 4.896 4.351	0.977@
Verbal Originality	109 158 133	468.660 457.765 449.142	123.093 143.757 108.096	0.705@
Total Verbal Creativity	109 158 133	620.018 606.107 596.458	150.595 176.444 135.203	0.678@
Non-verbal Fluency	109 158 133	48.146 46.063 47.827	10.962 11.968 10.116	1.435@
Non-verbal Flexibility	109 158 133	31.990 31.373 32.368	4.761 5.584 4.629	1.434@
Non-verbal Originality	109 158 133	241.908 231.170 240.375	59.611 59.083 50.240	1.490@
Total Non-verbal Creativity	109 158 133	322.045 308.607 320.571	73.799 75.537 63.676	1.511@
Composite Fluency	109 158 133	154.283 149.176 150.601	31.981 37.932 29.228	0.701@
Composite Flexibility	109 158 133	77.210 76.600 76.909	6.910 8.586 7.150	0.691@
Composite Originality	109 158 133	710.568 688.935 689.517	161.792 177.254 132.760	0.575@
Total Composite creativity	109 158 133	942.063 914.714 917.029	193.913 221.491 166.255	0.610@

CREATIVITY-FACTOR—N

Table 5.24: Means and SDs of Creativity Scores of Student Teachers of DIETs with Different Levels on Factor-N of 16 PF (Low: N_1-93; Moderate: N_2-147; High: N_3-160)

	N	*M*	*SD*	*F*
Verbal Fluency	93 147 160	106.709 101.591 104.200	28.973 28.844 25.457	1.006@
Verbal Flexibility	93 147 160	45.473 44.503 45.175	4.781 4.863 4.237	1.463@
Verbal Originality	93 147 160	465.741 452.170 458.525	133.394 134.833 116.128	0.327@
Total Verbal Creativity	93 147 160	617.924 598.265 607.900	163.164 166.167 143.637	0.455@
Non-verbal Fluency	93 147 160	46.709 46.258 48.393	11.727 11.383 10.454	1.543@
Non-verbal Flexibility	93 147 160	31.182 31.598 32.525	4.867 5.366 4.849	2.418@
Non-verbal Originality	93 147 160	234.924 234.115 241.250	62.601 57.444 51.864	0.704@
Total Non-verbal Creativity	93 147 160	312.817 311.972 322.168	77.870 73.042 65.801	0.920@
Composite Fluency	93 147 160	153.418 147.849 152.593	31.981 37.932 29.228	0.701@
Composite Flexibility	93 147 160	76.655 76.101 77.700	7.735 8.199 7.045	2.982@
Composite Originality	93 147 160	700.665 686.285 699.775	173.641 167.856 142.053	0.384@
Total Composite Creativity	93 147 160	930.741 910.237 930.068	210.045 209.255 176.722	0.534@

It is concluded that the Factor 'M' of 16PF has no significant influence on the creativity of student teachers of DIETs.

The Student Teachers who scored low, tend to be forth right, natural and sentimental than the teachers who scored high tend to be shrewd and polished. It is evident from the table the low group student teachers of DIETs exhibited higher mean scores on the three dimensions of verbal creativity <Fluency, Flexibility, Originality> Similarly with regard to non-verbal creativity the high group student teachers appeared as superior.

Consequently with regard to composite creativity on all the three dimensions as well as on the total composite creativity both low and high group student teachers scored higher mean scores of creativity than the middle group of factor 'N' of 16 PF. But these differences were not statistically significant as the calculated *F* ratios in all the situations were far below the table values even at 0.05 level of probability for 2,397 df. Therefore the null hypothesis that 'there exists no significant influence of factor N of 16 PF on creativity of student teachers of DIETs' is accepted. Hence, it is concluded that factor 'N' is not sharing with creativity.

The Student Teachers who scores low on factor 'O' tends to be placid, calm, with unshakable nerve, who scored high were depressed, moody, a worrier, suspicious, brooding, avoiding people. The factor 'O' of 16 PF speaks about the individual trait of confident Vs insecure. An observation into the mean values depicted in table reveals that there is no clear trend either in verbal, non-verbal or in composite creativity.

The obtained *F* values also could not reach the table value even at 0.05 level of probability for 2,397 df. Therefore the null hypothesis that 'there exists no significant influence of factor 'O' of 16 PF on creativity of student teachers of DIETs' is accepted. It is concluded that the factor 'O' of 16PF has no significant influence on the creativity of student teachers of DIETs.

The student teachers who scored low on factor 'Q_1' have the qualities of conservative and tolerant of traditional difficulties, than the high group of student teachers of experimenting, critical and free thinking.

Creativity-Factor—O

Table 5.25: Means and SDs of Creativity Scores of Student Teachers of DIETs with Different Levels on Factor-O of 16PF (Low: N_1-137; Moderate: N_2-113; High: N_3-150)

	N	*M*	*SD*	*F*
Verbal Fluency	137 113 150	104.036 101.805 105.153	29.512 27.625 25.726	0.480@
Verbal Flexibility	137 113 150	45.109 44.539 45.240	5.131 4.136 4.443	0.804@
Verbal Originality	137 113 150	461.109 446.345 463.586	139.610 121.903 118.993	0.659@
Total Verbal Creativity	137 113 150	610.255 592.690 613.980	171.841 149.752 147.095	0.648@
Non-verbal Fluency	137 113 150	46.759 47.115 47.713	10.643 11.850 11.031	0.269@
Non-verbal Flexibility	137 113 150	31.489 31.778 32.293	5.279 5.121 4.828	0.927@
Non-verbal Originality	137 113 150	234.124 236.000 240.800	55.033 60.406 54.989	0.531@
Total Non-verbal Creativity	137 113 150	312.372 314.893 320.806	69.671 75.903 69.698	0.526@
Composite Fluency	137 113 150	150.795 148.920 152.866	35.591 34.146 31.397	0.422@
Composite Flexibility	137 113 150	76.598 76.317 77.533	8.405 7.111 7.387	1.335@
Composite Originality	137 113 150	695.233 682.345 704.386	170.815 161.194 146.484	0.789@
Total Composite Creativity	137 113 150	922.627 907.583 934.786	212.454 195.418 182.921	0.745@

CREATIVITY-FACTOR—Q1

Table 5.26: Means and SDs of Creativity Scores of Student Teachers of DIETs with Different Levels on Factor Q_1 of 16 PF (Low: N_1-154; Moderate: N_2-134; High: N_3-112

	N	M	SD	F
Verbal Fluency	154 134 112	105.103 102.209 104.000	30.733 25.347 25.593	0.397@
Verbal Flexibility	154 134 112	44.909 44.619 45.511	5.204 4.197 4.167	1.350@
Verbal Originality	154 134 112	468.597 447.455 455.571	142.022 113.388 120.709	1.016@
Total Verbal Creativity	154 134 112	618.610 594.283 605.142	175.838 140.458 146.618	0.871@
Non-verbal Fluency	154 134 112	47.500 46.798 47.330	12.173 10.624 10.227	0.149@
Non-verbal Flexibility	154 134 112	31.489 31.778 32.293	5.279 5.121 4.828	0.927@
Non-verbal Originality	154 134 112	239.383 234.776 236.946	59.927 53.959 55.042	0.238@
Total Non-verbal Creativity	154 134 112	318.675 313.544 316.142	76.196 68.112 68.931	0.184@
Composite Fluency	154 134 112	152.603 149.007 151.330	37.284 30.608 31.834	0.409@
Composite Flexibility	154 134 112	76.398 76.397 77.864	7.974 6.887 8.220	0.185@
Composite Originality	154 134 112	707.980 682.231 692.517	176.997 136.785 158.107	1.169@
Total Composite Creativity	154 134 112	937.285 907.827 921.284	220.218 171.924 190.640	0.952@

An observation into the mean values presented in table reveals that there was no clear trend either in verbal, non-verbal or composite creativity. On some dimensions the low group of factor 'Q_1', scored high creative scores and on some the high group scored high but these differences appeared to be only due to sampling fluctuations and not because of the variations in factor 'Q_1'.

The calculated *F* ratios in all the situations also reveal that these differences are not statistically significant as the obtained *F* ratios are far below the table value even at 0.05 level of probability for 2,397 df. Therefore the null hypothesis that 'there exists no significant influence of factor Q_1 of 16PF on creativity of student teachers of DIETs' is accepted. Thus, it could be concluded that the factor Q_1, of 16 PF could not significantly influence the level of creativity among the student teachers of DIETs.

The Factor Q_2 of 16 PF speaks about the individuals trait of uncontrolled Vs self controlled. The Student Teachers who scored low tends to be group dependent and sound followers who were treated as more creative than the teachers of self sufficient and those who discount public opinion. The mean values depicted in the table explains that there was a clear trend either in verbal, non-verbal and composite creativity. The low group on factor Q_2 scored high creative scores.

However the calculated *F* values were significant at 0.05 level of probability for 2,397 df only on verbal, originality and total verbal creativity on all other dimensions the differences were not significant. Therefore the null hypothesis that 'there exists no significant influence of Factor Q_2 of 16 PF on creativity of student teachers of DIETs' is accepted. Thus, it is concluded that the factor Q_2 of 16PF has significant influence on the level of creativity of student teachers of DIETs.

The factor Q_3 of 16PF speaks about the individuals trait of dependent Vs self sufficient. The student teachers who scored low tend to be self conflict and undisciplined than the teachers of controlled and socially precise (high scorers) An observation

Creativity-Factor—Q2

Table 5.27: Means and SDs of Creativity Scores of Student Teachers of DIETs with different levels on Factor Q_2 of 16 PF (Low: N_1-112; Moderate: N_2-130; High: N_3-158)

	N	*M*	*SD*	*F*
Verbal Fluency	112 130 158	108.383 100.400 103.411	27.882 27.846 26.836	2.572@
Verbal Flexibility	112 130 158	45.410 44.630 45.006	4.511 4.870 4.455	0.861@
Verbal Originality	112 130 158	485.598 443.430 450.088	129.818 129.598 120.669	3.854*
Total Verbal Creativity	112 130 158	639.392 588.461 598.506	159.911 159.728 148.886	3.584*
Non-verbal Fluency	112 130 158	47.651 46.492 47.506	10.000 11.348 11.705	0.413@
Non-verbal Flexibility	112 130 158	32.169 31.546 31.930	4.508 5.111 5.411	0.470@
Non-verbal Originality	112 130 158	240.714 233.384 237.740	53.507 57.280 58.110	0.518@
Total Non-verbal Creativity	112 130 158	320.535 311.423 317.177	66.932 72.083 74.090	0.511@
Composite Fluency	112 130 158	156.034 146.892 150.917	33.316 35.964 31.867	0.935@
Composite Flexibility	112 130 158	77.579 76.176 76.936	6.554 8.286 7.844	2.326@
Composite Originality	112 130 158	726.312 676.814 687.828	155.720 161.792 157.540	3.000@
Total Composite Creativity	112 130 158	959.927 899.884 915.683	193.448 200.795 193.564	2.888@

CREATIVITY-FACTOR—Q_3

Table 5.28: Means and SDs of Creativity Scores of Student Teachers of DIETs with Different Levels on Factor-Q_3 of 16 PF (Low: N_1-136; Moderate: N_2-145; High: N_3-119)

	N	*M*	*SD*	*F*
Verbal Fluency	136 145 119	108.875 100.055 102.647	31.282 25.137 25.124	3.798*
Verbal Flexibility	136 145 119	45.426 44.620 44.966	5.128 4.397 4.210	1.077@
Verbal Originality	136 145 119	485.000 440.855 447.588	144.846 118.947 109.769	4.879**
Total Verbal Creativity	136 145 119	639.301 585.531 595.201	178.615 144.830 137.494	4.678**
Non-verbal Fluency	136 145 119	48.352 46.717 46.529	11.398 12.022 9.526	1.084@
Non-verbal Flexibility	136 145 119	32.191 31.600 31.840	5.594 4.851 4.703	0.479@
Non-verbal Originality	136 145 119	243.051 235.931 231.916	59.236 59.939 48.297	1.287@
Total Non-verbal Creativity	136 145 119	323.595 314.248 310.285	74.698 75.585 61.514	1.192@
Composite Fluency	136 145 119	157.227 164.772 149.176	37.574 32.049 29.703	3.632*
Composite Flexibility	136 145 119	77.617 76.220 76.806	7.891 7.451 7.727	0.958@
Composite Originality	136 145 119	728.051 676.786 679.504	178.202 156.080 133.345	4.462*
Total Composite Creativity	136 145 119	962.896 899.779 905.486	221.498 189.518 168.160	4.288*

into the mean values depicted in table reveals that there was a clear trend either in verbal, non-verbal and composite creativity. The low personality group student teachers on factor Q_3 scored high creative scores.

However the obtained *F* values were significant at 0.05/ 0.01 level of probability for 2.397 df only on verbal fluency, originality and total verbal creativity and composite fluency, originality and total composite creativity. Therefore the null hypothesis that 'there exists no significant influence of Factor Q_3, 16PF on creativity of student teachers of DIETs' is not accepted on the above dimensions and accepted with regard to non-verbal creativity and in composite flexibility. Thus, it is concluded that the personality factor Q_3 of 16PF has partial influence on the level of creativity of student teachers of DIETs.

The factor Q_4 of 16PF speaks about the individuals trait of stable Vs Tense. The person who scores low tends to be calm relaxed composed than the high scorers who tend to be tense, excitable, restless, and impatient. An observation into the mean values depicted in table reveals that 'there is no clear trend either in verbal, non-verbal or in composite creativity.

The calculated *F* ratios in all the situations also reveal that these differences are not statistically significant as the obtained *F* ratios are far below the table values even at 0.05 level of probability for 2,397 df. Therefore the null hypothesis that 'there exists no significant influence of factor Q_4 of 16PF on creativity of student teachers of DIETs' is accepted. Thus it could be safely concluded that the factor Q_4 of 16PF could not significantly influence the level of creativity among the student teachers of DIETs.

From the tables it is learnt that among the 16 personality factors only B, E, G, L, Q_2 and Q_3 could bring significant influence on creativity of student teachers. Therefore, the major null hypothesis that 'the 16 personality factors of student teachers of DIETs would not significantly influence their creativity' was not accepted in the case of first six factors and was accepted in the case of the remaining 10 factors.

CREATIVITY-FACTOR—Q_4

Table 5.29: Means and SDs of Creativity Scores of Student Teachers of DIETs with Different Levels on Factor-Q_4 of 16PF (Low: N_1-122; Moderate: N_2-105; High: N_3-173)

	N	*M*	*SD*	*F*
Verbal Fluency	122 105 173	105.000 100.657 104.919	27.975 28.977 26.394	0.940@
Verbal Flexibility	122 105 173	45.237 44.342 45.225	4.763 4.571 4.506	1.439@
Verbal Originality	122 105 173	471.106 451.904 452.150	135.773 137.681 113.441	0.952@
Total Verbal Creativity	122 105 173	621.344 596.904 602.294	165.824 169.417 141.249	0.806@
Non-verbal Fluency	122 105 173	47.688 46.352 47.410	10.805 11.800 10.946	0.451@
Non-verbal Flexibility	122 105 173	31.868 31.381 32.173	5.082 5.825 4.544	0.797@
Non-verbal Originality	122 105 173	240.860 232.428 237.416	56.028 59.819 54.905	0.630@
Total Non-verbal Creativity	122 105 173	320.418 310.161 317.000	70.184 76.406 69.271	0.598@
Composite Fluency	122 105 173	152.688 147.009 152.329	33.943 35.964 31.867	0.935@
Composite Flexibility	122 105 173	77.105 75.398 77.398	7.016 8.234 7.778	1.256@
Composite Originality	122 105 173	711.966 684.332 689.566	165.385 173.730 145.062	0.939@
Total Composite Creativity	122 105 173	941.762 907.065 919.294	204.001 215.848 179.057	0.819@

PREDICTION OF CREATIVITY

Prediction of Verbal Creativity with the help of all the Personal, Socio-psychological Variables Included in the Study

In this part the verbal creativity of student teachers of DIETs was predicted with the help of all the 26 variables, namely personal, demographic, achievement motivation, scientific attitude and 16 psychological characteristics. The means and standard deviations of all the variables measured and the simple correlations between each one of these independent variables and the dependent variable namely verbal creativity are depicted in the table.

The table indicates that out of 26 variables 8 variables are significantly correlated with verbal creativity. Among the personal and demographic variables age, sex, family literacy index, occupation of the father and annual income of the family of student teachers are significantly related with the dependent variable. The other three variables which had significant relationships with verbal creativity are achievement motivation, factor-L and factor Q_2 of 16 personality factors. Again out of 8 significant correlation co-efficients only one i.e., the correlation between sex and verbal creativity was significant at 0.01 level of probability for 399 df.

However, the inter correlations among the dependent variables would decide the order of their entry into the prediction equation depending upon their contribution to verbal creativity. The stepwise regression analysis was carried out to explain the variance in verbal creativity to the maximum extent possible with the help of predictor variables listed above. The summary of each step of the multiple regression analysis (the output of computer analysis) is given in table.

The first variable entered into the stepwise multiple regression analysis was 'sex' (S) of the student teachers of DIETs in predicting the verbal creativity (VC). The multiple correlation 'R' was 0.495 which was nothing but the simple correlation between sex and verbal creativity. It mean the strength of relationship was about 49%. The coefficient of multiple determination R^2 disclosed that about 24.5% of the variance in verbal creativity was accounted for by sex alone. The standard

Table 5.30: Means and SDs of independent variables and the simple correlations between the each one of the independent variables and dependent variable

Sl. No.	*Name of the Variable*	*Mean*	*SD's*	*Simple Correlation (r) with verbal Creativity*
1.	Education	1.550	0.498	–0.101
2.	Age	21.380	2.393	–0.245*
3.	Sex	1.500	0.501	0.495**
4.	Birth Order	2.248	1.438	–0.000
5.	Locality	1.325	0.469	0.111
6.	Family Literacy Index	7.965	4.206	0.233*
7.	Occupation of the Father	2.078	0.780	0.200*
8.	Annual Income	37.370	31.796	0.112*
9.	Achievement Motivation	50.278	3.981	0.122*
10.	Scientific Attitude	92.165	18 793	–0.086
11.	16PF factor A	8.265	2.450	–0.069
12.	Factor B	3.713	1.382	–0.044
13.	Factor C	6.855	2.367	–0.024
14.	Factor E	6.068	2.099	–0.092
15.	Factor F	6.395	2.174	–0.017
16.	Factor G	7.610	2.514	0.005
17.	Factor H	6.263	2.358	–0.034
18.	Factor I	5.585	2.159	–0.012
19.	Factor L	5.848	1.966	-0.108*
20.	Factor M	5.788	2.006	–0.046
21.	Factor N	5.975	1.964	0.008
22.	Factor O	6.570	2.367	–0.004
23.	Factor Q_1	6.045	1.977	–0.045
24.	Factor Q_2	5.508	1.795	–0.134*
25.	Factor Q_3	5.933	1.983	–0.075
26.	Factor Q_4	5.923	1.941	–0.066
27.	Verbal Creativity	606.690	156.588	

Table 5.31: Multiple (stepwise) Regression Analysis: Dependent Variable: Verbal Creativity; Independent Variables, Personal, Demographic and Psychological Variables

Step No.	Independent variable equated in each step	Multiple correlation 'R'	R^2	Standard error of multiple estimate	F.ratio d.f. & level of significance	Partial regression coefficient (b)	't' value for (b)	Constant	Bets Coefficient	Simple correlation coefficient with dependent variable	% of variance in the dependent variable explained by each variable
1.	Sex (S)	0.495	0.245	136.260	128.930** (1,398)	154.720	11.355**	374.61	0.495	0.495	24.5%
2.	Ach. Moti (AM)	0.512	0.263	134.758	70.871** (2,392)	155.868	11.562**	104.427	0.498	0.122	24.6%
						5.340	3.150**		0.136		1.7%
3.	16 PF-Q_2 (FQ_2)	0.524	0.275	133.855	50.010** (3,396)	154.035	11.486**	157.385	0.492	–0.134	24.3%
						5.375	3.191**		0.136		1.7%
						–9.436	2.524*		–0.108		1.5%
4.	Sci Athi. (SA)	0.530	0.281	133.438	38.615** (4,395)	154.297	11.541**	222.495	0.493	–0.086	24.4%
						5.252	3.126**		0.133		1.6%
						-9.436	2.435*		–0.104		1.4%
						-0.665	1.867@		–0.079		0.7%
5.	16PF G (FG)	0.534	0.285	133.191	31.497** (5,394)	155.036	11.610**	198.644	0.496	0.055	24.4%
						5.102	3.037**		0.129		1.5%
						–9.025	2.422*		–0.103		1.3%
						–0.683	1.922@		–0.082		1.0%
						4.71	1.568@		0.067		0.3%
6.	Occupation (O)	0.537	0.289	133.014	26.659 (6,393)	149.636	10.798**	183.371	0.478	0.200	23.5%
						4.944	2.941**		0.125		1.5%
						–9.292	2.495*		–0.106		1.4%
						–0.628	1.759@		–0.075		1.0%
						4.305	1.619@		0.069		0.3%
						12.814	1.432@		0.063		1.2%

error of multiple estimate 136.260 revealed that about 69% of the obtained verbal creativity scores would lie with in the range of ± 136.260 units of predicted verbal creativity scores.

The partial regression coefficient presented in column (7) was 154.720. This value indicated that verbal creativity (VC) increased by 154.720 units for every unit increase in sex. The 't' value for partial regression coefficient 11.355 was significant at 0.01 level. The constant value to be considered in equation was 374.610. Thus the equation at the end of the first step would be.

The general form of the prediction equation may be given as.

$$x^1 = A + b_1x_1 + b_2x_2 + b_3x3 + \dots\dots\dots + b_nx_n$$

Where, x^1 denotes the predicted score of dependent variable, 'A' is the constant. b_1, b_2, b_3.....bn are partial regression coefficients and x_1, x_2, x3.....xn are the obtained values on different independent variables. Thus the actual equation at the end of the first step would be.

$$VC_1 = 374.610 + 154.720\ S \dots\dots(1.1)$$

Achievement Motivation (A.M) was entered into regression analysis as the second most significant variable. The multiple correlation obtained between Verbal Creativity (VC) on one side and the two independent variables viz.... Sex (S) and Achievement Motivation (AM) on the other side was 0.512 which revealed that the strength of relationship between the dependent variable and the two independent variables put together was about 51.2%. The 'F' value obtained in the test for significance of multiple 'R' was 70.871 for 2,397 df. The two variables put together could explain 26.4% (R^2=0.263) of variance in the verbal creativity. Out of this 26.4% of the variance explained by the two predictor variables, the contribution of Sex (S) was 24.7% and the Achievement Motivation (AM) could account for about 1.7% of the variance in verbal creativity. The percentages were obtained by multiplying the β-coefficients. (Standard Partial Coefficients Column 10) with the corresponding simple correlations between the dependent variable and the respective independent variables.

The partial regression coefficients of S and AM were 155.868 and 5.340 respectively and they were significant at 0.01 level and the constant at this stage was 104.427. The regression equation to predict VC, with S and AM as predictor variables was

$$VC = 104.427 + 155.868\ S + 5.340\ AM \quad ......(1.2)$$

In the hierarchy of predictor variables associated with VC, factor Q2 (FQ_2) entered as the next important variable. The multiple correlation or the combined association of S, AM, FQ_2 with VC, was 0.524 and the multiple determinant 0.275 was significant at 0.01 level (F=50.010 for 3,396 df). The value of R^2=0.275 disclosed that about 27.5% of the variance in Verbal Creativity (VC) was explained by these three variables. Out of 27.5% of total variance, explained in VC by these three variables put together 24.4% was accounted by S, 1.7% by AM and 1.5% by FQ_2.

The partial regression coefficients at this step revealed that for every unit increase in S, AM, FQ_2 the VC, would increase by 154.035, 5.375 and -9.436 units respectively. The first two partial regression coefficients were significnt at 0.01 level and the third was significant at 0.05 level. (t = 11.486, 3.191 and 2.524). The regression equation at this step with the constant of 157.385 was.

$$VC = 157.385 + 154.035\ S + 5.375\ AM + -9.436\ FQ_2 \quad ......(1.3)$$

The fourth variable entered into the step wise regression analysis was Scientific Attitude (SA). The multiple 'R' was 0.530 which was significant at 0.01 level. It revealed that the combined strength of relationship between the bunch of independent variables viz.. S, AM, FQ_2 and SA was 53%. Thus the increase in 'R' was not much (0.006). All the four variables put together could explain 28.1% of variance in the verbal creativity. It was observed that, by Scientific Attitude (SA) as one more predictor variable in the analysis and it could increase the total variance explained in the dependent variable from 52.4% to 53%. The changes in these values from the earlier step was due to inter correlations between the predictor variables.

Among the four partial regression coefficients the first two one were significant at 0.01 level (t = 11.541, 3.126), while the third one was significant at 0.05 level (t = 2.435). The lost coefficient was not significant even at 0.05 level. The constant value to be considered in the equation was 222.495. The regression equation which would predict the verbal creativity at this step was

$$VC = 222.495 + 154.297\ S + 5.252\ AM + -9.436\ FQ_2 + -0.665\ SA \quad ......(1.4)$$

In the hierarchy of predictor variables associated with verbal creativity, Factor 'G' entered as the fifth important variable. The multiple correlation or the combined association of S, AM, FQ_2, SA and FG was 0.534 which was significant at 0.01 level (F = 31.497 for 5,394 df). The value of $R^2 = 0.285$ disclosed that about 28.5% of the variance in verbal creativity was explained by these five variables. The 't' value for partial regression coefficients of the first three were significant either at 0.05 or at 0.01. The constant being 198.644, the equation was

$$VC = 198.644 + 155.036\ S + 5.102\ AM + -9.025\ FQ_2 + -0.683\ SA + 4.71 FG \quad ......(1.5)$$

The last significant predictor variable that entered into the analysis was Occupation of the father (O). All the six variables put together explain 28.5% of the variance in the dependent variable 'VC'. The multiple determinant and all the partial regression coefficients of all the variables except 'SA', 'FG' and 'O' were significant either at 0.05 or at 0.01 levels. The regression equation with the six predictor variables could be written as follows:

$$VC = 183.371 + 1493636\ 'S' + 4.944\ AM + -9.292\ FQ_2 + -0.628\ SA + 4.305\ FG + 12.814\ 'O' \quad ......(1.6)$$

Out of the six regression equations formulated above, the three most important variables which contribute to verbal creativity were sex, achievement motivation and factor Q_2. The other variables viz., scientific attitude, factor G of 16 PF and Occupation of the father could also enter into the analysis but their contributions to the dependent variable were not significant. The first three variables which could explain about 27.5% of the variance in the verbal creativity might be treated as the best equation to predict the dependent variable verbal creativity.

Prediction of Non-verbal Creativity with the help of the Personal, Socio-psychological Variables Included in the Study

In this part the non-verbal creativity of student teachers of DIETs was predicted with the help of all the 26 variables namely personal and demographic, achievement motivation, scientific attitude and 16 psychological characteristics. The means and standard deviations of all the variables measured and the simple correlations between each one of these independent variables and the dependent variable namely non-verbal creativity are depicted in the table.

The table indicates that out of 26 variables 10 variables were significantly correlated with non-verbal creativity among the personal and demographic variables sex, locality, family literacy index, occupation of the father and Annual Income of the family of student teachers were significantly related with the dependent veriable. The other five variables which had significant relationship with non-verbal creativity are Factor-C, Factor-G, Factor-L, Factor-N and Factor-Q_2 of 16 personality factors. Again out of 10 significant correlation coefficients only one i.e., the correlation between sex and non-verbal creativity was significant at 0.01 level of probability where as the other nine were significant at 0.05 level of probability for 399 df.

However the inter correlations among the dependent variables would decide the order of their entry into the prediction equation depending upon their contribution to non-verbal creativity. The stepwise regression analysis was carried out to explain the variance in non-verbal creativity to the maximum extent possible with the help of predictor variables listed above. The summary of each step of regression analysis is presented in table.

The first variable entered into the analysis was sex (S). The multiple correlation at this step was nothing but the simple correlation itself (r=R=0.480). It means the strength of the relationship was about 48%. The multiple 'R' was significant beyond 0.01 level for 1 and 398 df. The coefficient of multiple determination R^2 was 0.230. It means roughly about 23% of the variance in the non-verbal creativity of student teachers of DIETs was being explained by 'Sex'.

Table 5.32: Means and SDs of Independent Variables and the Simple Correlations Between the each one of the Independent Variables and Dependent Variable

Sl. No.	*Name of the Variable*	*Mean*	*SD's*	*Simple Correlation (r) with non-verbal Creativity*
1.	Education	1.550	0.498	–0.145
2.	Age	21.380	2.393	–0.186
3.	Sex	1.500	0.501	0.480**
4.	Birth Order	2.248	1.438	0.054
5.	Locality	1.325	0.469	0.121*
6.	Family Literacy Index	7.965	4.206	0.270*
7.	Occupation of the Father	2.078	0.780	0.162*
8.	Annual Income of the Father	37.370	31.796	0.124*
9.	Achievement Motivation	50.278	3.981	–0.049
10.	Scientific Attitude	92.165	18.793	–0.060
11.	16 PF factor A	8.265	2.450	–0.007
12.	Factor B	3.713	1.382	–0.132
13.	Factor C	6.855	2.367	0.045*
14.	Factor E	6.068	2.099	–0.038
15.	Factor F	6.395	2.174	–0.050
16.	Factor G	7.610	2.514	–0.095*
17.	Factor H	6.263	2.358	–0.087
18.	Factor I	5.585	2.159	0.028
19.	Factor L	5.848	1.966	–0.112*
20.	Factor M	5.788	2.006	–0.038
21.	Factor N	5.975	1.964	0.059*
22.	Factor O	6.570	2.367	0.059
23.	Factor Q_1	6.045	1.977	–0.024
24.	Factor Q_2	5.508	1.795	–0.091*
25.	Factor Q_3	5.933	1.983	–0.060
26.	Factor Q_4	5.923	1.941	–0.029
27.	Verbal Creativity	316.248	71.408	—

Table 5.33: Multiple (stepwise) Regression Analysis: Dependent Variable: Non-verbal Creativity; Independent Variables, Personal, Demographic and Psychological Variables

Step No.	*Independent variable equated in each step*	*Multiple correlation 'R'*	R^2	*Standard error of multiple estimate*	*F.ratio d.f. & level of significance*	*Partial regression coefficient (b)*	*'t' value for (b)*	*Constant*	*Beta Coefficient*	*Simple correlation coefficient with dependent variable*	*% of variance in the dependent variable explained by each variable*
1	**2**	**3**	**4**	**5**	**6**	**7**	**8**	**9**	**10**	**11**	**12**
1.	Sex (S)	0.480	0.230	62.736	118.923** (1,398)	68.415	10.905**	213.625	0.480	0.480	23%
2.	Family Literacy Index (FLI)	0.491	0.242	62.289	63.679** (2,397)	62.566 2.045	9.444** 2.593**	206.109	0.438 0.120	0.162	21% 3.2%
3.	16PF Factor L (FL)	0.498	0.249	62.105	43.825** (3,396)	61.738 2.055 –2.906	9.325** 2.613** 1.832@	224.266	0.432 0.121 –0.080	–0.112	20.7% 3.2% 1.0%
4.	Factor N (FN)	0.504	0.257	61.918	33.917** (4,395)	61.536 2.057 -3.617 2.993	9.321** 2.624** 2.223* 1.843@	210.823	0.431 0.121 –0.009 0.082	–0.059	21% 3.2% 1.1% 0.4. %
5.	Factor G (FG)	0.511	0.262	61.727	27.990** (5,394)	61.172 2.050 -3.512 3.270 –2.297	9.290** 2.623** 2.163* 2.011* 1.856@	226.637	0.428 0.120 –0.096 0.090 –0.080	–0.095	20.5% 3.2% 1.0% 0.5% 1.0%

(Contd...)

Table 5.33: (Contd...)

1	2	3	4	5	6	7	8	9	10	11	12
6.	Factor C (FC)	0.516	0.267	61.560	23.976**	61.465	9.357**	213.783	0.430	0.045	20.8%
					(6,393)	2.054	2.636**		0.121		3.2%
						–3.315	2.043*		–0.091		0.3%
						3.160	1.947*		0.086		0.9%
						–2.898	2.264*		–0.102		1.0%
						2.402	1.773*		0.079		0.5%
7.	Factor Q (FQ)	0.521	0.270	61.456	20.953**	61.155	9.321**	223.046	0.428	–0.091	20.5%
					(7,392)	2.033	2.613**		0.119		3.2%
						–2.623	1.559@		–0.072		0.8%
						3.706	2.223*		0.102		0.6%
						–3.008	2.350*		–0.105		1.0%
						2.470	1.825@		0.081		0.3%
						–2.827	1.525@		–0.071		0.6%
8.	Factor I	0.526	0.274	61.295	18.814**	60.963	9.315**	219.935	0.427	0.028	20.5%
					(8,391)	2.007	2.585**		0.118		3.1%
						–3.847	2.116*		–0.105		1.1%
						3.339	2.001*		0.091		0.5%
						–3.032	2.375*		–0.106		1.0%
						2.427	1.797@		0.080		0.3%
						–3.297	1.765@		–0.082		0.7%
						2.867	1.751@		0.086		0.2%
9.	Factor B	0.531	0.278	61.170	17.080**	59.286	8.965**	232.298	0.415	–0.132	19.9%
					(9,390)	2.068	2.667**		0.121		3.2%
						–3.918	2.159*		–0.107		1.2%
						3.341	2.006*		–0.091		0.5%
						–2.732	2.122*		–0.096		0.9%
						2.498	1.853@		0.082		0.3%
						-3.449	1.847@		-0.086		0.7%
						3.204	1.944@		0.096		0.2%
						-3.702	1.612@		–0.071		0.9%

The partial regression coefficient 68.415 indicated that the non-verbal creativity increased by 68.415 units for every unit increase in sex. The 't' value for partial regression coefficient was significant beyond 0.01 level (t = 10.905). The constant value to be considered in the equation was 213.625. Thus the equation at the end of the first step would be

NVC = 213.625 + 68.415 S ......(2.1)

In the second step the additional predictor variable that entered into the regression analysis was Family Literacy Index (FLI). The multiple 'R' was 0.491 which revealed that the strength of relationship between the dependent variable and the two independent variables viz., sex and family literacy index (FLI) was about 49.1%. The 'F' value obtained 63.679 was significant for 2,397 df. These two variables put together could explain 24.2% of variance in the dependent variable. Out of 24.2% of variance in the dependent variable. Out of 24.2% of the variance explained by the two predictor variables, the contribution of S was 21% and the FLI could account for about 3.2% of the variance in non-verbal creativity. These values were obtained by multiplying the ß-coefficients of 'S' and FLI with their simple correlations. 0.438 and 0.120 with the dependent variable respectively and they were significant at 0.01 level.

The reduction in the variance explained by 'S' from 23% to 21% was due to the inter correlation between S and FLI. The constant at this stage was 206.109. Thus the regression equation at the end of this step could be written as:

NVC = 206.109 + 62.566 S + 2.045 FLI ......(2.2)

In the hierarchy of predictor variables associated with NVC, Sex (S) 16 personality Factor 'L' entered as the next important variable. The combined or cumulative strength of association between these three predictor variables i.e., S, FLI and FL with NVC, was 0.498 and the multiple determinant 0.249 was significant at 0.01 level. Out of 24.9% of total variance explained in NVC by these three variables put together 20.7% was accounted for by 'S', 3.2 by FLI, and 1.0% by FL. All the three partial regression coefficients at this step revealed that for every unit increase in 'S', FLI and FL, the NVC would increase by 61.738, 2.055, and –2.906 units respectively. The two (S, FLI), coefficients were found to be, significant at 0.01 level (t=9.325, 2.613) and the 'β' coefficients of FL was not significant even at 0.05 level. The constant value was 224.266. The regression equation to predict NVC with the help of three variables could be written as:

NVC = 224.266 + 61.738 'S' + 2.055 FLI + –2.906 FL ......(2.3)

16 personality Factor 'N' (FN) was the next variable entered into the stepwise regression analysis. The multiple R, 0.504 indicated that the strength of the relationship between NVC and a bunch of 4 predictor variables as 50.4%. The multiple determinant which was significant at 0.01 level discloses that these four variables put together could explain 25.7% of the variance in the dependent variable, out of this 21.6% was accounted for by 'S', 3.2% by FLI, 1.1% by FL, and 0.4% by FN. The changes in these values from the earlier step was due to intercorrelations between the predictor variables. The first three partial regression coefficients were significant either at 0.05 or at 0.01 level and the fourth was not significant. The constant was 210.823. Thus the equation at this step could be written as:

NVC = 210.823 + 61.536 S + 2.057 FLI + –3.617 FL
+ 2.993 FN ......(2.4)

The fifth variable in the hierarchy of the predictor variables entered into the analysis was Factor 'G' (FG). The strength of the relationship was about 51% (R=0.511). The bunch of these predictor variables put together could explain 26.2% of the variance in non-verbal creativity out of this 20.5% was accounted for by 'S', 3.2% by FLI, 1.0% by FL, 0.5% by FN and 1.0 by FG. The changes in these values from the earlier step was due to intercorrelations between the predictor variables. The '*t*' value for partial regression coefficient of all the variables except FG were significant either at 0.01 or at 0.05 level. The constant was 226.637. Thus the equation at this step was.

NVC = 226.637 + 61.172 S + 2.050 FLI + –3.512 FL + 3.270 FN
+ -2.297 FG ......(2.5)

Factor 'C' (FC) entered as the next predictor variables in the analysis and it could increase the total variance explained in the dependent variable from 26.2% to 26.7%. The '*t*' value for partial regression coefficients of all the variables except FN and

FC were significant either at 0.05 or at 0.01 levels. The regression equation at this step could be written as:

$$NVC = 213.783 + 61.465\,S + 2.054\,FLI + -3.315\,FL + 3.160\,FN + -2.898\,FG + 2.402\,FC \;......(2.6).$$

Factor Q_2 (FQ_2) entered as the next predictor variable in the analysis and it could increase the total variance explained in the dependent variable from 26.7% to 27%. The multiple 'R' 0.521 indicated that the strength of the relationship between NVC and a bunch of 7 predictor variables as 52.1%. The multiple determinant which was significant at 0.01 level discloses that these seven variables put together could explain 27% of the variance in the dependent variable NVC. The '*t*' value for partial regression coefficients of all the variable except FLI, FC and FQ_2 were significant either at 0.01 or at 0.05 levels. The constant was 223.046. The equation at the end of this stage was.

$$NVC = 223.046 + 61.155\,S + 2.033\,FLI + -2.623\,FL + 3.706\,FN + -3.008\,FG + 2.470\,FC + -2.827\,FQ_2 \;......(2.7).$$

Factor 'I' (FI) entered as the next predictor variable in the analysis and it could increase the total variance explained in the dependent variable from 27% to 27.4%. The partial regression coefficients of all the variables except FC, FQ_2 and FI were significant either at 0.05 or at 0.01 levels. The constant value was 219.935. The regression equation at this step could be written as:

$$NVC = 219.935 + 60.963\,S + 2.007\,FLI + -3.847\,FL + 3.339\,FN + -3.032\,FG + 2.427\,FC + -3.297\,FQ_2 + 2.867\,FI \;......(2.8)$$

The last significant predictor variable that entered into the analysis was the Factor-'B' (FB). All the 9 variables put together could explain 27.8% of the variance in the dependent variable NVC. The multiple determinant and all the partial regression coefficients of all the variables except FG, FC, FQ_2, FI and FB were significant either at 0.05 or at 0.01 levels. The regression equation with the 9 predictor variables could be written as follows:

$$NVC = 232.298 + 59.286\,S + 2.068\,FLI + -3.918\,FL + 3.341\,FN + -2.732\,FG + 2.498\,FC + -3.449\,FQ_2 + 3.204\,FI + -3.702\,FB \;......(2.9)$$

Although there were seven personality factors significantly correlated with non-verbal creativity (NVC) none of them could enter into regression analysis as predictor variables probably due to insignificant contribution they could make to non-verbal creativity. Out of nine regression equations formulated above, equation number 2.5 considered to be the best equation as it could explain 26% of the variance in NVC.

Prediction of composite creativity with the help of the personal Socio-Psychological variables included in the study

In this part the composite creativity of student teachers of DIETs was predicted with the help of all the 26 variables namely personal, demographic psychological characteristics. The means and standard deviations of all the variables measured and the simple correlations between each one of these independent variables and the dependent variables namely creativity are depicted in the table.

The table explains that out of 26 variables among the personal and demographic variable, sex, locality, family literacy index, occupation of the father and Annual income of the family of student teachers are significantly related with the dependent variable. The other three variables which had significant relationships with creativity are scientific attitude, Factor-N and Factor-Q_2 of 16 personality factors. Again out of 8 significant, correlation coefficients only one i.e., the correlation between sex and creativity was significant at 0.01. Where as the other seven were significant at 0.05 levels of probability for 399 df.

However, the inter correlations among the dependent variables would decide the order of their entry into the prediction equation depending upon their contribution to creativity. The stepwise regression analysis was carried out to explain the variance in creativity to the maximum extent possible with the help of predictor variables listed above. The summary of each step of the multiple regression analysis (the out put of computer analysis) is given in table.

The step wise regression analysis was carried out to explain the variance in creativity to the maximum extent possible with the help of personal, demographic variables, personality factors

Table 5.34: Means and SDs of Independent Variables and the Simple Correlation Between each one of the Independent Variables and Dependent Variable

Sl. No.	*Name of the Variable*	*Mean*	*SD's*	*Simple Correlation (r) with Creativity*
1.	Education	1.550	0.498	–0.121
2.	Age	21.380	2.393	–0.251
3.	Sex	1.500	0.501	0.560**
4.	Birth Order	2.248	1.438	0.023
5.	Locality	1.325	0.469	0.130*
6.	Family Literacy Index	7.965	4.206	0.275*
7.	Occupation of the father	2.078	0.780	0.212*
8.	Annual Income	37.370	31.796	0.131*
9.	Achievement Motivation	50.278	3.981	0.086
10.	Scientific Attitude	92.165	18.793	–0.077*
11.	16 PF Factor A	8.265	2.450	–0.047
12.	Factor B	3.713	1.382	–0.088
13.	Factor C	6.855	2.367	0.008
14.	Factor E	6.068	2.099	–0.079
15.	Factor F	6.395	2.174	–0.036
16.	Factor G	7.610	2.514	0.017
17.	Factor H	6.263	2.358	–0.057
18.	Factor I	5.585	2.159	–0.002
19.	Factor L	5.848	1.966	–0.120
20.	Factor M	5.788	2.006	–0.046
21.	Factor N	5.975	1.964	0.036*
22.	Factor O	6.570	2.367	0.022
23.	Factor Q_1	6.045	1.977	–0.052
24.	Factor Q_2	5.508	1.795	–0.137*
25.	Factor Q_3	5.933	1.983	–0.077
26.	Factor Q_4	5.923	1.941	–0.065
27.	Creativity	921.193	196.837	—

in creativity as Predictor Variables. The contribution of each Predictor Variable in explaining the variance in Creativity was also calculated and discussed. The summary of step wise regression analysis of the output of computer analysis is presented in Table 5.35.

The first Variable entered into the analysis was sex (s) of the student teachers of DIETs. The multiple correlation at this step was nothing but the simple correlation itself [r=R=0.559]. It mean the strength of relationship about 55.9%. The coefficient of multiple determination R^2 was 0.313. It means roughly about 31.3% of the variance in the creativity of the student teachers of DIETs being explained by the 'Sex'.

The partial regression coefficient 220.235 indicated that creativity increased by 220.235 units for every unit increase in sex of the student teachers of DIETs. The 't' value for partial regression coefficient 13.489 was significant at 0.01 level. The constant value to be considered in the equation was 590.840. Thus the equation at the end of the first step would be.

$$C = 590.840 + 220.235\,S \quad ......(3.1)$$

16 personality Factor Q_2 [FQ_2] entered in regression analysis as the second most significant variable. The multiple correlation obtained between creativity [c] on one side and the two independent variables viz..... sex [s] and 16PF Factor Q_2 [FQ_2] on the other side was 0.570 which revealed that the strength of relationship between the dependent variable and the two independent variables put together was about 57%. The two variables put together could explain 32.5% [R^2=0.325] of variance in the creativity. Out of this 32.5% of the variance explained by the two predictor variables, the contribution of sex[s] was 31% and the FQ_2 account for about 1.5% of the variance in creativity. The percentage was obtained by multiplying the ß-coefficients (Standard partial coefficients) column [No-10] with the corresponding simple correlations between the dependent and the respective independent variables.

The partial regression coefficients of S and FQ_2 were 217.953 and –11.700 respectively and they were significant at 0.01 level and the constant at this stage was 658.700. The regression

Table 5.35: Multiple (Step-Wise) Regression Analysis: Dependent Variable: Composite Creativity; Independent Variables: Personal, Demographic and Psychological Variables

Step No.	Independent variable equated in each step	Multiple correlation 'R'	R^2	Standard error of multiple estimate	F.ratio d.f. & level of significance	Partial regression coefficient (b)	't' value for (b)	Constant	Beta Coefficient	Simple correlation coefficient with dependent variable	% of variance in the dependent variable explained by each variable
1	2	3	4	5	6	7	8	9	10	11	12
1.	Sex (S)	0.559	0.313	163.265	181.962** (1,398)	220.235	13.489*	590.84	0.560	0.560	31.3%
2.	16 PF-Q (FQ_2)	0.570	0.325	162.112	95.618** (2,397)	217.953 –11.700	13.424** 2.584**	658.700	0.554 -0.106	-0.137	31% 1.5%
3.	Achievement Motivation (AM)	0.578	0.335	161.065	66.637** (3,396)	219.018 –11.792 5.036	13.573** 2.621** 2.485*	404.380	0.557 –0.107 0.101	0.086	31.2% 1.5% 0.8%
4.	Family Literacy Index (FLI)	0.585	0.343	160.282	51.687* (4,395)	206.237 –11.649 5.106 4.483	12.083** 2.602** 2.532* 2.209*	383.526	0.524 -0.106 0.103 0.095	0.275	29.3% 1.5% 0.9% 2.6%

(Contd...)

Table 5.35: (Contd...)

1	2	3	4	5	6	7	8	9	10	11	12
5.	16PF Factor.N (FN)	0.589	0.347	159.979	42.006**	205.875	12.083**	359.183	0.523	0.036	29.3%
					(5,394)	-13.639	2.938**		-0.124		1.7%
						5.026	2.496*		0.101		0.9%
						4.468	2.205*		0.095		2.6%
						6.696	1.580$^{@}$		0.066		0.2%
6.	Factor.N (F̂L)	0.592	0.351	159.712	35.508**	204.323	11.991**	384.964	0.519	-0.120	29.1%
					(6,393)	−11.687	2.430*		-0.106		1.5%
						4.982	2.478*		0.100		0.8%
						4.503	2.226*		0.096		2.6%
						7.785	1.814$^{@}$		0.077		0.2%
						−6.630	1.522$^{@}$		−0.066		0.9%
7.	Scientific Attitude (SA)	0.595	0.355	159.404	30.914**	205.61	12.076**	458.270	0.522	−0.077	29.2%
					(7,392)	−11.003	2.283*		−0.100		1.4%
						4.851	2.416*		0.098		0.8%
						4.106	2.018*		0.087		2.4%
						7.414	1.729$^{@}$		0.074		0.2%
						−7.290	1.669$^{@}$		−0.072		0.9%
						−0.685	1.587$^{@}$		−0.065		0.6%

equation to predict 'C' with S and FQ_2 as predictor variables was:

$$C = 658.700 + 217.953 \text{ 'S'} + -11.700 \ FQ_2 \ ......(3.2)$$

In the hierarchy of predictor variables associated with creativity [c], Achievement Motivation [AM] entered as the next important variable. The multiple correlation or the combined association of S, FQ_2, AM with 'C' was 0.578 and the multiple determinant 0.335 was significant at 0.05 level F=66.637 for 3,396 df. The value of R^2=0.335 disclosed that about 33.5% of the variance in creativity [c] was explained by these three variables. Out of 33.5% of total variance explained in 'creativity 31.2% was accounted for by 's' 1.5% by FQ_2, 0.8% by AM.

The partial regression coefficients at this step revealed that for every increase in 'S' FQ_2, AM the 'C' would increase by 219.018, -11.792 and 5.036 units respectively. The three partial regression coefficients were significant either at 0.01 level or at 0.05 level [t=13.573, 2.621, 2.485]. The regression equation at this step with the constant of 404.380 was:

$$C = 404.380 + 219.018 \text{ 'S'} + -11.792 + 5.036 \ ......(3.3)$$

Family Literacy Index [FLI] was the next variable entered into the step-wise regression analysis. The multiple 'R' 0.585 indicated that the strength of the relationship between creativity [c] and a bunch of four predictor variables was 58%. The multiple determinant which was significant at 0.01 level disclosed that these four variables put together could explain 34.3% of the variance in the dependent variable. Out of this 29.3% was accounted for by 'S', 1.5% by FQ_2, 0.9% by AM, 2.6 by FLI. The changes in these values from the earlier step was due to inter-correlations between the predictor variables. All the four partial regression coefficients were significant either at 0.05 or at 0.01 levels. The constant was 383.526. Thus, the equation at this step was:

$$C = 383.526 + 206.237 \text{ 'S'} + -11.649 \ FQ_2 + 5.106 \ AM + 4.483 \ FLI \ ......(3.4)$$

Factor-N [FN] was the next variable entered into the regression analysis. The multiple 'R' was 0.589. The total variance that could be explained in the dependent variable by the host of five variables was 34.7%. The '*t*' value for partial regression coefficients of all the variables except Factor-N were significant either at 0.05 or at 0.01 level. The constant being 359.183, the equation was written with all the five predictor variables as:

$$C = 359.183 + 205.875\ 'S' + -13.639\ FQ_2 + 5.026\ AM + 4.468\ FLI + 6.696\ FN \quad ......(3.5)$$

The next variable entered into the regression analysis was Factor-L [FL]. The multiple 'R' was significant and the strength of the relationships was 59.2% between creativity and the host of six predictor variables. The bunch of these six predictor variables put together could explain 35.1% [R^2=0.351] of the variance in creativity. The '*t*' values for partial regression coefficients of all the variables except Factor-N [FN] Factor-L [FL] were significant either at 0.05 or at 0.01 level. The constant being 384.964 the equation was written with all the six predictor variables as:

$$C = 384.964 + 204.323\ 'S' + -11.687\ FQ_2 + 4.982\ AM + 4.503\ FLI + 7.785\ FN + -6.630\ FL \quad ......(3.6)$$

The last significant predictor variable that entered into the analysis was Scientific Attitude [SA]. All the seven variables put together could explain 59.5% of the variance in the dependent variable creativity. It could increase the total variance explained in the dependent variable from 59.2% to 59.5%. The 't' value for partial regression coefficients of all the variables except FN, FL, SA were significant either at 0.05 or at 0.01 level. The regression equation with the seven predictor variables could be written as follows:

$$C = 458.270 + 205.610\ 'S' + -11.003\ FQ_2 + 4.851\ AM + 4.106\ FLI + 7.414\ FN + -7.290\ FL + -0.685\ SA \quad ......(3.7)$$

However, the last three variables could not have significant partial regression co-efficients. Therefore the equation number 3.4 considered to be the best equation as it could explain almost 34.3% of the variance in creativity with significant contributions by each of the four variables.

☆ ☆ ☆

6

Summary and Conclusions

SUMMARY

Creativity is a kind of psychic wonder. Creative talent makes history through reshaping man's world. Creativity is mankind's greatest asset. Creativity is a distinguishing characteristic of outstanding individuals in almost every field.

Butcher (1972) observed 'Any society to avoid stagnation, needs constant supply of original ideas at all levels but profoundly original men who are the most fertile source of these ideas are often the vary people who most disturb the society by threatening its estabiished ways of thought and familiar structure.

Creativity has been defined variously, it consists in uniqueness. It is thinking in divergent directions. Creative products are novel constructs. This novelty is a result of his interaction with the materials of his environment in divergent ways.

There are two modes of intellectual operations, convergent thinking and divergent thinking. Divergent thinking leads to creativity. While creativity is one of the most highly valued human qualities.

All development in any sphere of activity in the nation, springs from the way creativity is fastened and encouraged among boys and girls in the schools. Creativity in schools is not in consistent with the daily work in the class room for. It planned imaginatively all work in the school can stimulate and encourage children into creative thinking and turn the process of learning in to an enjoyable experience to both the teacher and taught and incidentally, enrich the whole education in the country.

Creativity to say the least is mankind's greatest asset. It is an ability that is most vital for the shaping of man's future. The basic feature of creativity is curiosity to explore, examine and understand nature to find new facts yet unexplored. This is in deed the key to the advancement of our knowledge. The main motive of creativity is to create something tangible and new.

The human world has progressed only with creative abilities in man. These abilities should be identified and developed systematically, and used for the progress of mankind. Education, indeed has a pivotal role in the identification and nourishing of such creative talents.

Today the focus of the entire world is on this specialised area 'creativity'. Research in the field of creativity has been an outcome of this realisation. The present interest in the creative or inventive process through which the mind produces new and useful ideas arises from a growing realisation of the importance of new ideas for the success of an individual.

Statement of the Problem

The present study is stated as follows: Creativity: It correlates of certain personal, social, psychological variables of student teachers of 'DIETs'. This study is designed to investigate into various factors of 'creativity' and the influence of probable intervening variables on creativity.

Objectives of the Study

The main objectives of the study are:

1. to study the level of creativity among student teachers of DIETs;
2. to study the influence of personal and social variables on creativity;
3. to study the influence of psychological variables on creativity;
4. to predict creativity with the help of a selected bunch of independent variables.

Hypothesis

1. The general level of creativity among student teachers of DIETs is normal.

2. The personal and demographic variables of student teachers of DIETs would not bring any significant influence on their creativity (each variable will be tested independently).

3. The psychological variables such as—Achievement motivation, scientific Attitude, and 16 personality factors of student teachers of DIETs would not significantly influence their creativity (each variable will be tested independently).

4. It would not be possible to predict creativity (verbal, non-verbal or both) with the, help of personal, social and psychological variables.

Variables Studied

The dependent variable in the study is creativity of student teachers of DIETs. The independent variables are broadly grouped under Personal and demographic variables and Psychological variables and Personality characteristics.

Creativity

Creativity involves the ability to produce original ideas and to perceive new relationships among unrelated things. However, it does involve just an ability to produce original ideas. Creativity is multifaceted.

(i) Personal and demographic variables: Under this category the following variables were studied:

1. Sex	5. Locality
2. Qualifications	6. Birth Order
3. Age	7. Occupation
4. Family Literacy Index	8. Annual Income.

(ii) Psychological Variables: - 1. Achievement Motivation.
2. Scientific Attitude Test.

(iii) Personality Characteristics

Cattell's 16 personality factors were considered to study the impact of personality of the student teachers on the dependent variable, namely creativity.

1.	Factor-A	–	Aloof vs Warm, outgoing
2.	Factor-B	–	Dull vs Bright
3.	Factor-C	–	Emotional vs Mature
4.	Factor-E	–	Submissive vs Dominant
5.	Factor-F	–	Glum, Silent vs Enthusiastic
6.	Factor-G	–	Casual vs Conscientious
7.	Factor-H	–	Timid vs Adventurous
8.	Factor-I	–	Tough vs Sensitive
9.	Factor-L	–	Trustful vs Suspecting
10.	Factor-M	–	Conventional vs Eccentric
11.	Factor-N	–	Simple vs Sophisticated
12.	Factor-O	–	Confident vs Insecure
13.	Factor-Q_1	–	Conservative vs Experimenting
14.	Factor-Q_2	–	Dependent vs Self-controlled
15.	Factor-Q_3	–	Uncontrolled vs Self-controlled
16.	Factor-Q_4	–	Stable vs Tense.

Measurement of Variables

To measure student teachers creativity, creative thinking is judged on the basis of the verbal, non-verbal and composite creativity scores obtained on all the components of creativity i.e., (fluency, flexibility, originality).

To measure the achievement motivation a test developed by 'Rao' was adopted in the present investigation. As the instrument was a multi-dimensional test and proved its Universal applicability, the instrument was considered valid.

To measure scientific attitude of student teachers of DIETs a test developed by Prof. Venkatarami Reddy in Telugu the regional language of Andhra Pradesh State was used. It contains 40 items, 20 positive and 20 negative.

The 16 personality traits were measured by adopting Form-C of the 16-PF questionnaire developed by Cattell. The instrument was translated carefully and used.

The data regarding personal and demographic variables were obtained with the help of personal data sheet prepared separately for the purpose.

Sample

To measure creativity of student teachers of DIETs. Students belonging to District Institute for Education and Training (DIETs) located in Rayalaseema Region of Andhra Pradesh State are selected at random. A total of 400 Ss for the study equally distributed between two sexes and the four DIETs, was the sample.

Data Collection

The subjects were administered the instruments under normal classroom conditions in small groups of not exceeding 20 at a time. After establishing proper rapport, they were told about the nature and importance of the work so as to motivate them to take the tests in a right spirit. Before administering each sub-test, the students were explained what they had to do with the help of the example given in the instructions for each sub-test.

The creativity tests were administered in the morning session giving a gap of 15 minutes after the first 7 sub-tests. Achievement motivation, Scientific attitude and 16 personality factors (Form-C) scale were administered giving a gap of 10 minutes after completion of each test. All the instruments were administered as per the instructions given in the respective manuals which were explained in Telugu the regional language of the subjects.

Scoring

Much care was taken in scoring the responses for the items in creativity tests as there is no right or wrong response. To enhance the objectivity of scoring the usual procedure adopted is to get the responses scored by different scorers and to see that the inter scorer reliability is high.

The responses of the Ss were scored based upon the following procedure suggested by Guilford (1951) Torrance (1962) Child (1973) and Venkatarami Reddy and Balakrishna Raddy (1983) etc.,

Achievement motivation, scientific attitude, Cattell 16 personality factors (from-C) were scored as per the procedure given in the respective manuals.

The information provided by the respondents in the personal data were also numerically coded to suit the computer analysis.

Analysis

The data were carefully analysed by employing appropriate statistical techniques such as *'t'* test, and *F* test etc., to know the effect of independent variables on creativity.

The stepwise regression analysis was adopted to predict creativity with the help of all the personal, demographic and psychological variables as predictors.

MAJOR FINDINGS AND CONCLUSIONS

On the basis of the results obtained in the investigation the following conclusions were drawn.

1. The existing level of verbal creativity among the student teachers of DIETs is above average level.
2. The existing level of non-verbal creativity among the student teachers of DIETs is above average level.
3. The existing level of composite creativity among the student teachers of DIETs is also above average level.

It is observed that the student teachers of DIETs are moderately creative—a positive sign. This status is probably due to by entrance test which is a competitive one that is being administered on the candidates and the rank obtained by them is considered as the basis for their admission in to D.Ed., programme conducted by the DIETs. But are they conscious about their creative ability and whether they are being trained in developing creativity among the students whom they are going to teach are not known.

4. The student teachers with suitable qualifications are more creative than the over qualified student teachers of DIETs.

5. The appropriate age group of student teachers are more creative than the older age group of student teachers of DIETs.

6. The female student teachers are more creative than the male student teachers of DIETs.

7. Birth order has no significant influence on the creativity of student teachers of DIETs.

8. The Urban student teachers are more creative than the rural.

9. The Family Literacy Index has significant bearing on the creativity of the student teachers of DIETs.

10. Secured job group of student teachers are more creative than the other counterparts.

11. Annual Income has no significant influence on the creativity.

Thus among eight personal and demographic variables birthorder and Annual Income, did not significantly influence, the creativity of student teachers of DIETs on the other hand variables like qualifications, age, sex, locality, Family Literacy Index and occupation of the father were found to be significantly influencing the creativity of the student teachers of DIETs.

It is observed that the student teachers of suitably qualified at appropriate age and female from Urban areas, having better family literacy index are proved to be superior in creativity than their counterparts. The over qualified and over aged are naturally entered in to teaching profession as a last resort and there by they were not as much creative as their counterparts. Similarly the female student teachers were found to be superior over male candidates even by considering the number of candidates admitted in D.Ed., programme the larger contingent is from these groups. It is a favourable trend and this is because of the competitive entrance that is being conducted for the purpose of admitting into D.Ed. programme.

12. There exists no significant difference among low, moderate and high achievement motivation groups of student teachers in their creativity.
13. There exists no significant difference between low, moderate and high scientific attitude groups of student teachers in their creativity.
14. Personality factor 'A' of 16PF could not significantly influence the level of creativity.
15. Factor-B, intelligence could bring significant influence on the creativity of student teachers of DIETs.
16. Factor 'C' of 16 PF could not significantly influence the level of creativity.
17. Personality factor-E of 16 PF has significant influence the level of creativity of student teachers of DIETs.
18. Factor-F of 16PF has no bearing on the creativity of student teachers of DIETs.
19. Factor-G of 16 PF has significant influence on creativity among the student teachers of DIETs.
20. Factor 'H' could not bring any significant influence on the creativity of student teachers of DIETs.
21. High group on Factor-I appeared to be more effective in their creativity than the middle and low group student teachers altogether the differences were not significant.
22. Factor-L has significant influence on the level of creativity among the student teachers of DIETs.
23. Factor-M was not a significant personality factor in influencing the creativity of student teachers of DIETs.
24. The low and high group of student teachers of factor-N appeared to be more effective in their creativity than

the middle group but the variations were not significant.

25. The factor-O of 16PF has no significant influence on the creativity.

26. The high scores on factor-Q_1 appeared to be more creative than the middle and low groups of student teachers. However, the differences were not statistically significant.

27. The high group of student teachers on factor-Q_2 were significantly more, creative than the middle and low groups.

28. Factor-Q_3 of 16 PF has partial influence on the level of creativity of student teachers of DIETs.

29. Factor Q_4 of 16PF also did not exhibit any significant bearing on the creativity of student teachers of DIETs.

Thus out of 16 personality factors only five factors i.e., B, E, G, L, and Q_3 could influence the creativity of student teachers of DIETs significantly.

Among the personality characteristics low general ability (B^+), submissive (E^+), conscientious (G^+) self opinionated (L^+) self conflict (Q_3^+) were associated with more creativity, while the opposite poles of these characteristics were associated with less creativity.

30. It could be possible to predict verbal creativity of student teachers of DIETs, with the help of personal, demographic and psychological variables. As much as 27.5 per cent of the variance in verbal creativity was accounted for by a bunch of '6' independent variables.

31. To predict non-verbal creativity of student teachers of DIETs with the help of personal, demographic and psychological variables. As much as 26% of the variance in non-verbal creativity was accounted for by a bunch of 9 independent variables.

32. It could be possible to predict creativity of student teachers of DIETs with the help of personal,

demographic and psychological variables. As much as 34.3 per cent of the variance in composite creativity was accounted for a bunch of 7 independent variables.

The creativity is multifacted, complex variable with all the 26 independent variables included in the study it could be possible to explain only one third of the variance in creativity. This phenomenon itself explains how complex and multifaceted the creativity is: Further research is essential in this direction to identify the other independent variables which can contribute more to the creativity, so as to make us to identify innovative strategies, for the development of the creativity among the younger generations.

EDUCATIONAL IMPLICATIONS

Educators are legitimately concerned that their students make useful contributions to the society. Such concern runs deep in the code of ethics of the profession. It takes little imagination to recognise that the future of our civilization, depends upon the quality of the creative imagination of our next generations.

Creativity is the life and blood of human civilazation. The future of our nation depends upon the creative talents of the future citizens of our society. Therefore creativity has rightly become a chief psycho-social motif of the present century. Creativity is the highest type of mental functioning, multivariate and complex. Every child is creative to some extent. It is wide spread and it manifested in numerous ways. It is educabie and its growth can be accelerated.

Eberle (1968) found that the influence of training in creative thinking processes is significantly reflected in the personality factors of adolescents. Therefore, it is essential that the aims of education, curriculum, method of teaching, promotions and rewards should be remodeled according to the needs of children. In order to promote and develop creative talent, the school programmes need modification. The teacher training colleges (DIETs) selection and promotion procedures of teachers and the system of administration will have to be overhauled with a view to stimulate potentialities of teachers who would be real guides for the creative students. The ultimate goal aim being that of bringing improvement in functional roles and group dynamics for promoting creative talent. Teachers should be trained to identify these personality factors among the children and develop programmes to foster them among the children.

It has been found that creative individuals are characterised by a wide latitude of flexibility of ideas. In our education system, the rigid curricula, lecture oriented teaching and examination system, dampens spart of creativity in children. Hence, we must create a more flexible educational system in which individuals should be provided with opportunities and encouragement needed for stimulating, nourishing creative thinking.

According to the report of the Indian Education Commission (1964) even the little talent that enters schools and succeeds in climbing the educational ladders, does not blossom fully because it is not discovered sufficiently early and is after engulfed in 'poor schools' poor with respect to the environment they provide to the children. Creative ability which is a true barometer of our present and future progress needs to be identified early and nurtured properly. But can it blossom in a vacuum? The necessity of favourable environment for its promotion can not be exaggerated. Therefore conditions congenial to creativity at home and in the school should be studied thorough and identified correctly.

Therefore, the present day student teachers are to be trained in identifying the creative abilities of the children and encourage them to develop further in the directions in which they can grow to the fullest extent possible. The in-service training programme should include this component as an inherent future of the teacher trainee. To achieve this goal the curriculum for the D.Ed. level has to be revised accordingly.

Creativity is more than word today. It is an incantination. It is a kind of psychic wonder (Singh, 1987). Creative talent makes history through reshaping man's world. Creative students are the most valuable national asset. Torrance (1962) has shown that both the educational system and teachers themselves are punitive towards children showing creative potential.

One of the main objective of any system of education is to help unfold and promote to the maximal possible extent the inherent potentialities of its clientele. These potentialities include, among many other things, the creative abilities which keep man above the brute. These are the abilities involved in becoming aware of problems, thinking possible solutions and testing them. If their functioning is impaired, one's capacity for coping with life's problems indeed becomes marginal (Torrance, 1962).

The human world has progressed only because of such creative abilities in man. These abilities should be identified and developed systematically, and used for the progress of mankind. The physical potentialities of any nation remain useless, until human potentialities like the creative abilities through their ingenuity knew how to exploit them.

Modern psychologists categorically assumed that

(i) Creativity is possessed by everyone in smaller or greater measure;

(ii) These abilities are capable of being developed and

(iii) Schools should shoulder the responsibility of such training.

Developmental psychology has shown us that creative process can be taught, but the state of affairs in our schools is such that creative students are dissatisfied with the schools and their programmes. Creativity is an essential factor in the effort to realise the national goals and schools are the place for discovering and developing creativity.

There are individual differences in the degree of creative thinking. The period of early childhood is marked by the rapid occurance of simple creative visions arising from naturalness. The creative images occur so rapidly that the children unaware of them. Further every child realises that each one of them can do some sort of original work, which is worthwhile in its own way. Therefore, the methods of teaching at primary level are to be thoroughly modified. The play way techniques, the project method, the heuristic method, and the experimental method are to be given top priority. While teaching children which will pack the creative ability of the children and encourage them to manifest their inherent creative talance and develop self learning skills among them. The principles of APEP (Andhra Pradesh Primary Education Project) and DPEP (District Primary Education Programme) are developed only to achieve this goal of tapping the creativity among the children.

It is the responsibility of colleges courses and teachers in education, to remove the erroneous belief that the creative work, teachers and their pupils can do is negligible. The teachers contact with the child is a very powerful agent in determining the way in which individuals will use their talents. Schools and colleges should endeavour to develop creativity of the students. The students should be urged to go further and do creative work.

Outside the class room parents can also do much to foster creative thinking in the child. Parents should always be alert to notice the child's creative work and give him proper guidance and assistance.

In the schools curricular should be flexible for students to comeup. Creativity is something like a pearl in an oyster and so has to be brought up. So the text books will have to make provision for more opportunities for creative learning. If it is considered a worth while objective.

The teacher should always give positive reinforcement to their thinking. New ideas should always be encouraged. Teachers should pose problems having more than one solution and encourage alternative solutions. Children should be encouraged to complete their assignments and experiments in their own way. Pupils should not be hurried on their projects, they should be given ample time to think of all the alternative solutions. Through encouragements, acceptance and respect for the student's creative responses, an atmosphere could be created which would be generally responsive, that could build and sustain the students in creative work

Schools can chalkout programmes to nourish the creativity of children. It is with in their reach because, it has been found that creativity is developable through flexible curriculum, the democratize administration through student's councils and committees. Scientific and recreational hobbies, magazines, writing competitions, painting competitions, debates, poetical symposia, excursions, tours etc., go a long way in developing the creative potential of children.

This will be possible only when the teachers are made aware of the creative teaching process and its effect on pupils growth. This may necessitate in pre-service training courses in creative teaching practices. If teachers are trained in such techniques, they will have a significant influence on the productivity of the children interns of fluency, flexibility, originality and other creativity factors.

LIMITATIONS AND FURTHER RESEARCH

1. The study included only 400 student teachers of four DIETs of Andhra Pradesh. Similar study may be conducted on a larger population of different regions in Andhra Pradesh.

2. Only a few independent variables are included in the present study, the relation between creativity and other affective variable like values, level of adjustment, aspirations, vocational interest, etc., many such variables may be considered in the further research studies.

In measuring the personality of student teachers of DIETs two forms of 16 PF should be used to attain more stable results. But in the present study only one form was employed because of the use of several other data gathering instruments. The future researchers may use at least two forms of 16 PF and the results may be compared.

India is a multilingual, multicultural, multiracial country. A comparative study of the creativity of the students belonging to different cultures and different races would be very fascinating to unravel cultural and racial effects on creativity. Further are students belonging to bilingual localities more creative than those hailing from unilingual localities? A study on this may be worth while.

That creativity of lecturers is no less important than that of students can not be denied. But how creative are the lecturers working in the DIETs? The present study was limited to students only. No attempt was made to study the creativity of the lecturers and its effect on the creativity of the student teachers of DIETs. A study on this aspect may be, very useful to the educational administrators in devising ways of enhancing the creativity of the students since it is only the creative lecturer that can fruitfully implement creative programmes in the DIETs.

Bibliography

Ashok, K. Kalia. 1985. Creativity correlates of intelligence academic achievement and extroversion neuroticism. *Journal of Educational Research and Extension*, 21, 4, 214-222.

Arnold, J.E. 1962. Useful creative techniques, (In) Parnes, S.J. and Harding, H.F.(Eds) *A source book for creative thinking*, Charles Serifner's Sons, New York, 251-268.

Arnold, J.E. 1963. Creative imagination: A course in mechanical engineering. *Paper presented at Regional meeting of ASEE University of Vermountfall*, Mimeographed.

Awasthy, M. 1979. A study of creativity intelligence, scholastic achievement and the factors of socio-economic status *Unpublished M.Ed., dissertation*, Indore University, Indore.

Agarwal, S.C. and Gupta, S.P. 1982. A study of biographical attributes of high and low creative student teachers *Indian Education*, 12, 8.

Andrews, E.G. 1930. The development of imagination in the preschool child. *University of Iowa Studies of Character*, 3, 1-64.

Ahmed, S. 1980. Effect of socio-cultural disadvantage on creative thinking. *Journal of Psychological Researches*, 24, 2, 96-106.

Aaron, P.G., Marihal, V.G. and Malatesha, A.N. 1969. The rural and urban school—*A comparative study of the Socio-Psychological conditions of the pupils and the teachers*. Dept. of Edn, Karnataka University, 98-99.

Bharadwaj, R. 1985. Intelligence, sex and age as correlates of the components of creativity. *Asian Journal of Psychology and Education*, 16, 3, 41-44.

Bharadwaj, R. and Sharma, A.D. 1986. Intelligence, fixation, frustration and economic status as corelates of the originality. *Journal of Educational Psychology*, 44, 2 and 3, 158-161.

Bloom, B.S. (Ed) 1958. Some effects of cultural, Social and Educational conditions on creativity (In) Calvin, W. Taylor (Ed). *The second*

(1957) *University of Utah Research Conference on the Identification of Creative Scientific Talent*, University of Utah Press, 55-65.

Burns, M.J. 1969. Selected characteristics of children's individuals tests of creativity. *Dissertation Abstracts International*, 30, 5, 1859A.

Burt, C. 1962. Introduction, *The Gifted Child*, (In): Beredy, G.Z.F. and Laurways, J.A. (Eds) *The Gifted Child. Brace and World*, New York.

—— 1964. Forward (In) Koestler, A. *The Act of Creation*, Hatchinson, London.

Burgess, W.V. 1971. The analysis of teacher creativity, pupil age and pupil sex as sources of variation among elementary pupil's performance on pre and post tests of creative thinking. *Dissertation Abstracts International*, 32, 2, 747.

Buhl, H.R. 1960. *Creative Engineering Design, Iowa State University Press, Iowa.*

Brodley, F.K. 1976. The effect of frustration on the figural creativity thinking of 5th grade students. *Journal of Experimental Education*, 44, 3, 20-23.

Buhl, H.R. 1961. Understanding the creative Engineer, *American Society of Mechanical Engineers*, New York.

Badrinath, S. and Satyanarayana, S.B. 1979. Correlates of creative thinking of high school students. *Creativity News Letter*, 7-8, 2 & 1, 16-23.

Barron, F. 1958. The psychology of imagination, *Scientific American*, 199, 151-666.

——1961. Creativity: What research says about it, *NEAJ*, 50, 17-19.

Barron, F. 1965. The psychology of the creative writer. *Paper presented at the Annual meeting of the American Psychological Association, Chicago.*

—— 1969. Creative person and creative process, New York, Holt, *Rinehart and Winston*, Inc., New York.

Bajpai, A. and Ahmed, A.1986.A study of creativity in relation to anxiety and level of aspiration in male and female teacher trainees. *M.Ed. Dissertation Abstract*, Devi Ahalya Visvavidyalayam, Indore.

Cattell, R.B. and Butcher, J. 1968. The prediction of achievement and creativity Indianapolis, *Ind. Bobbs-Merrill.*

Cattell and Drevdahl, J.C. 1955. A comparison of the personality profile (16PF) of eminent researchers with that of eminent teachers and administrators, and of the general population. *British Journal of Psychology*, 46, 248-261.

Cacha, F.B. 1971. A study of creative thinking abilities of personality factors and peer nominations of fifth grade children. *Dissertation Abstracts International*, 32, 3, 1329A.

Cattell, R.B. 1956. Second order personality factors in the questionnaire realm. *Journal of Consulting Psychology*, 20, 411-418,

—— 1963. The personality and motivation of the researcher from measurements of contemporaries and fr m biography. Ch.9 (In) Taylor and Barron (Eds) *Scientific Creativity: Its Recognition and Development John Wiley and Sons*, New York, 119-131.

Chadha, N.K. and Ghose, P. 1985. Sex differences in creativity risk taking, intelligence and frustration: An inferential study, *Journal of Educational Research and Extension*, 21, 4

Chaplin, J.P. 1982. *Dictionary of Psychology*, Dell, New York.

Child, D. 1973. *Psychology and the Teacher*. London: Rinehart and Winston Holf.

Child, D. and Croucher, A. 1977. A divergent thinking and ability: Is there a threshold. *Educational Studies*, 3, 101-110.

Chandrakant, Bhogayata, 1987. The effect of birth order, sex and urban-rural dimensions of culture on creativity of secondary school students. *Journal of Education and Psychology*, 44, 4, 212-216.

Colvin, S.S. and Meyer, I.F. 1906. Imaginative elements in the written work of school children. *Pedagogical Seminary*, 13, 17-28.

Csikszentmihalyi, 1964

Crutchfield, R.S. 1967. Instructing the individual in creative thinking (In) Ross, L. Mooney and Taher, A. Razik (Eds) *Explorations in Creativity*. Harper and Row, New York, 196-205.

Cheek, J.F. 1979. An analysis of differences in creative ability between white and Negro students, public and parochial, three different grade levels and males and females. *APA Experimental Publication System*, 9, Ms. No.349-54.

Dexie, F. 1985. Test of creative thinking potentials, academic achievement, 7th –12th graders- *Information of Psychological Sciences*, 2, 20-25.

Doppett, 1964. What is creativity? III. Definitions of creativity. Transactions, *Academy of Sciences*, New York, 26, 788-793.

Drevdahl, J.E. 1956. Factors of importance for creativity. *Journal of Clinical Psychology*, 12, 21-26.

——1964. Some developmental and environmental factors in creativity (In) Taylor, C.W. (Ed.) *Widening Horizons in Creativity*, John Wiley and Sons, Inc., New York, 170-185.

Dharmagandan, B.C. 1976. Creativity in school children: An analytical study. *Unpublished Ph. D. Thesis,* University of Kerala, Trivandrum.

——— 1981. Creativity in relation to sex, age and locality. *Psychological Studies,* 26, 1, 28.33.

Dutt, N.K., Prem Bountra, and Sabharawal, V.K. 1977. A study of creativity in relation to intelligence, extraversion and neuroticism. *Indian Educational Review,* 8, 2, 81-87.

Eisenman, Russel, 1988. Creativity birth order and risk taking. *Bulletin of Psychonomic Society.*

Foster, J.1971. *Creativity and the Teacher.* Macmillan Education Ltd., London.

Fromm, E. 1959. The creative attitude (In) Anderson, H.H. (Ed) Creativity and its Cultivation, Harper and Row, New York, 44-54.

Freud. S. 1949. The unconscious (In) Jones, Earnest (Ed.) *collected papers,* 4, 98-139.

Flanagan, J.C. 1958. Definition and measurement of ingenuity (In) Taylor, C.W. (Ed.) The second university of Utah Research *Conference on the Identification of Creative Scientific Talent,* University of Utah Press, Salt Lake City, 109-118.

Flang, Dexie, 1985. Test of creative thinking potentials, academic achievement, 7th –12th graders. *Information of Psychological Sciences,* 2, 20-25.

Getzels, J.W. and Jackson, P.W. 1961. Family environment and cognitive styles: A study of the sources of highly intelligent and highly creative adolescents. *American Psychological Review,* 26, 351-359.

———1962. Creativity and Intelligence: *Explorations with Gifted Students,* John Wiley & Sons Inc., New York.

——— and Madaus, G.F. 1969. Encyclopedia of Educationl Research. *A project of the American Educational Research Association.* The Macmillan Company, Collier Macmillan Limited, London, 267-273.

Ginsberg, G.P. and Whittmore, R.G. 1968. Creativity and verbal ability. A direct examination of their relationship. *British Journal of Educational Psychology,* 38, 133-139.

Gray, 1954., Skinner, C.E. 1962. Essentials of Education (In) Venkateswaran, S. 1987. Academic achievement and creativity. *Journal of Educational Research and Extension,* 24, 52-58.

Griffiths, R.A. 1945. *A Study of Imagination in Early Childhood.* Routledge, London.

Grennancre, P. 1959. Play in relation to creative imagination: *Psychoanalytic Study of the Child,* 14, 61-80.

Golamn, S.E. 1961. Psychological study of creativity. *Psychological Bulletin*, 60, 548-565.

Goldenson, R.M. 1984. *Longman dictionary of psychology and psychiatry.* Awalter, D. Glanzebook, New York.

Ghiselin, B. 1952. The creative process. New American Library, 293.

Guilford and Hoepfner, R. 1966. Creative potential as related to measures of IQ and verbal comprehension. *Indian Journal of Psychology*, 41, 7-16.

—— 1962. Creativity: Its measurement and development (In) Parnes, S & J and Harding, H.P. (Eds). *A Source Book for Creative Thinking*, New York, Scribner, 151-168.

Guilford, J.P. 1950. Creativity. *American Psychologist*, 5, 9, 444-454.

—— 1952. Some recent findings on thinking abilities and their implications. T.A. & D. *Information Bulletin* U.S. Air Force, III, 3, 61.

——1954. *Psychometric methods*. Mc. Graw Hill, New York, 529-530.

——1956. The Structure of Intellect. *Psychological Bulletin*, 53, 267-293.

—— 1957. *A Revised Structure of Intellect*, (Rep. Psychol. Lab., No.19) University of Southern California, Los Angeles, 69-65.

—— 1959. Factors and Psychological Theory, *American Psychologist*, 434.

Gakhar, S. 1974. Creativity in relation to age and sex. *Journal of Education and Psychology*, 32, 3.

——1975. Intellectual and personality correlates of creativity. *Doctoral Thesis*, Punjab University.

Gallangher, J.J. 1963. A Conference on Research on the Education of Gifted children, Cooperative Research Project, No. F. 006, U.S. Dept. of Health, Education and Welfare, Washington, D.C.

Gagneja, S.L. 1972. A study of creativity in ninth class students in relation to sex, residential background, academic achievement and parental occupation. *Master's dissertation*, Punjab University.

Harnek, S., Kaile Gurusagar, Sadhu and Manjit, K., Sekhon, 1988. Creativity in relation of sex and birth order. *The Educational Review*, XCIV, 11, 195-197.

Hallman, R.J. 1963. The necessary and sufficient conditions of creativity. *Journal of Humanistic Psychology*, 3-1.

Hussain, M.G. 1974. Creativity and sex differences. *Psychological Studies*, 19, 2, 127-129.

—— 1976. Creativity and sex differences. *Psychological Abstracts*, 56, 1186.

Hatchinson, E.D. 1949. How to think creatively. Nashville: Abingdon Press, 97.

Hatchinson, W.L. 1967. Creative and productive thinking in the class room, *Journal of Creative Behaviour*, 1, 4, 419-427.

Jarial, Gurpal Singh, 1979. Verbal creative thinking among the students with different socio-economic status back-grounds and birth orders. *Psycho Lingua*, 9, 2, 85-90.

——1981. Effect of birth order upon creative thinking abilities among adolescents. *Psychological Studies*, 1981 (In Press).

—— 1981a. Creativity and family size. *Journal of Education and Psychology* (In Press).

——1983. Creativity and Family size, *Journal of Education*, 1, 1, 13-17.

——1981. Effect of personality types, grade levels and their interaction upon creativity and its components. *The Educational Review* (In Press).

—— 1981a. The effect of birth order upon intelligence. A review of studies. *Journal of the Institute of Educational Research*, 55, 30-33.

Jackson, R.L. 1968. An investigation of the creative growth curves of University Students. *Dissertation Abstracts*, 28, 9, 3508A.

Jha, S.K. 1978. (In) Passi, B.K. 1982. Creativity in Education, National Psychological Corporation, Agra.

—— 1978. An analysis of certain dimensions of creativity. Himalaya Publishing House, Bombay.

Jayaswal, V.K. 1977. A study of creativity in relation to anxiety in male and female teacher trainees. *Dotoral Thesis*. Gorakhpur University.

Joshi, F.E. 1964. A study of creativity and some personality traits of the intellectually gifted high school students. *Dotoral Thesis*, M.S University, Baroda.

Kloss, M.G. 1972. The relation between adolescent creativity and selected variables, sex, adjustment, art-science preference, complexity-simplicity, and type of school. *Dissertation Abstracts International*, 33, 5, 2324B.

Kogan,N.A. 1971. Clarification of Cropely and Maslany's analysis of the Wallach-kogan creativity tests. *British Journal of Psychology*, 62, 113-117.

Kour, R. 1978. Personality characteristics of high school creative children. *Unpublished M.A. (Ed.) Dissertation*, Punjab University.

Khatena, J.1973. Creativity, concept and challege. *Educational Trends*, 8, 7-18.

Khire, U.S. 1971. Creativity in relation to intelligence and personality factors. *Doctoral Thesis*, Poona University, Poona.

Kelly, G.R. 1965. Creativity, shool attitude and intelligence relationships in grades four, six and eight. *Dissertation Abstracts*, 25, 11, 6300.

Lalithamma, M.S. 1973. Self concept and creativity of over normal and under achievers amongst grade X students of Baroda city, *unpublished M.Ed., Dissertation*, M.S. University, Baroda.

Lehman, H.C. 1953. Age and Achievement, Princeton, New Jersey.

Lovell, K. and Shields, J.B. 1967. Some aspects of a study of the gifted children. *British Journal of Educational Psychology*, 37, 201-208.

Lowenfeld, V. 1957. Creativity and Mental Growth, Macmillan, New York.

Maccoby and Jacklin, C.N. 1974. *The Psychology of sex differences*, Stanford University Press, Stanford.

Mc Cloy, W. 1939. Creative imagination in children and adults. *Psychological Monographs*, 51, 88-102.

Mc Dowell, M.S. and Howe, S.R. 1941. Creative use of play materials by pre school children. *Childhood Education*, 17, 321-326.

Mac Gregor, M. and Smith, J.L. 1965. Originality and role perception in elementary and junior high school children. *Dissertation Abstracts*, 25, 11, 6762.

Machinnon, D.W. 1962. The natura and nurture of creative talent. *American Psychologist*, 17, 484-495.

Marsh, R.W. 1964. A statistical analysis of Getzels and Jacksons data. *British Journal of Educational Psychology*, 34, 91-93.

Maslow, H. 1963. The creative attitude. *The Structurist*, 3, 4-10.

Mason, J.G. 1960. How to be a more creative executive. Mc Graw Hill, New York.

Madaus, 1967. Quoted in Cauhan, N.S. and Tiwari. Manual of Creativity Test. *Agra Psychological Research Cell*, Agra.

Mehdi, B. 1973. Manual: *Verbal test of creative thinking*, Mrs. Qumar Fatima, Aligarh.

——1977. Creativity, intelligence, academic achievement. A relational study, *Psychological studies*, 22, 1.

Merrifield, P. 1976. How an educational psychologist use the creative process. *Educator*, 18, 2, 16, TEEN, 22 WO.

Morgan, E.S. 1960. What every yale freshman should knows *Saturday Review*, 43, 1-14.

Mednick, S.H. and Mednick, M.T. 1964. An associative interpretation of the creative process (In) Taylor, C.W. (Ed.) Widening Horizons in creativity. John Willey and Sons Inc., New York, 54-68.

Marsh, R.W. 1964. A statistical Analysis of Getzels and Jacksons data. *British Journal of Educational Psychology*, 34, 91-93.

Middents, G.J. 1968. The relationship of creativity and anxiety. *Dissertation Abstracts*, 28, 7, 2562A.

Nair, M. 1976. Personality characteristics of Creative High School Pupils. *Master's Thesis*, Kerala University, Trivandrum.

Newell, A. 1962 and others. The process of creative thinking (In) Graber, H.E. *et al.*, (Eds.) *Contemporary Approaches to Creative Thinking*, Altherton Press, 63-119.

Nunnally, J.O. 1959. Tests and measurements: *Assessment and Prediction.* Mc Grow Hill Book Company, New York.

NCERT- 1971. *'A study of attitude of teachers towards teaching profession data processing and educational survey unit"*, New Delhi Secondary Survey of Research in Education.

Olton, R.M. 1969. The development of productive thinking skills in fifth grade children. *Wisconsin Research and Development Centre for Cognitive Learning University of Wisconsin*, Madison.

Olshin, G.M. 1965. The relationship among selected subject variables and levels of creativity. *Exceptional Children*, 31, 588-589.

Ogletree, E.J.A. 1968. Cross cultural exploratory study of the creativeness of steiner and state school pupils in England, Scotland and Germany, *Dissertation Abstracts*, 29, 2, 516A.

——1971. A cross-cultural examination of the creative thinking ability of public and private school pupils in England, Scotland and Germany. *Journal of Social Psychology*, 83, 310-302.

—— 1972. Creative discontinuties of European school children. *The Journal of Social Psychology*, 88, 147-148.

Osborn, 1948. Applied imagination, New York, Charles Schibner's Sons (Indian Edition, Allahabad: St Paul Publications).

—— 1948. Your creative power: Now to use imagination, Charles Scribner's Sons, New York.

——1957. Creative imagination, 3rd Ed., Charles Scribner's Sons, New York.

Pogue, B.C. 1964. A study to determine whether or not there is a relationship between creativity and self image. *Doctoral Dissertation*, Bale State University.

Philips, V.K. and Torrance, E.P. 1971. Divergent thinking remote associations and concept attainment strategies. *Journal of Psychology*, 77, 223-228.

Phatak, 1962. Experimental study of creativity and intelligence and school achievements. *Psychological Studies*, 7, 1-9.

Pestonjee, D. and Usmani, S.M. 1982. Creativity in relation to alienation, ego strength and intelligence. *Journal of Education and Psychology*. 40, 1-2, 39-44.

Patel, A.S. and Joshi, R.J. 1976. An inquiry into the relation of creativity to intellectual giftedness. *A paper submitted to the Indian Science Congress*, Waltair.

Pandey, R.C. and Pandey, R.N. 1984. A study of creativity in relation to sex of high school students. *Indian Psychological Review*, 26, 2, 53-57.

Padmanabhaiah, S. 1984. "Job satisfaction and teaching effectiveness of secondary school teachers". *Doctoral Thesis*, S.V.University, Tirupati, A.P.India.

Pandit, R. 1976. A study of creativity in relation to adjustment socio-economic status and scholastic achievement of the students. *Unpublished M.Ed., Dissertation, Indore University, Indore.*

Passi, B.K. 1972. An exploratory study of creativity and its relationship with intelligence and achievement in school subjects as higher secondary stages. *Doctoral Thesis*, Punjab University.

—— 1979. *Passi Test of Creativity* (Verbal and Non-verbal). National Psychological Corporation, Agra.

—— 1982. *Creativity in Education* 1st edition National Psychological Corporation, Agra, 1-19.

—— and Lalithamma, M.S. 1973. Self concept and creativity of over, normal and under achievers amongst grade X students of Baroda. *Indian Journal of Psychometry and Education*, 4, 1, 1-11.

Patel, A.S. 1978. An enquiry in to the relation of creativity to intellectual giftedness. *Indian Journal of Psychology*, 53, 3, 140-144.

Parnes, S.J. 1966. Work book for creative problem solving institutes and courses, Creative Education Foundation, Buffalo.

Paramesh, C.R. 1970 and Narayanan, S. 1974. Creativity and Intelligence on temperament. *Journal of Education and Psychology*, 34, 3 and 4, 159-161.

Quereshi, Anjum Naseer, 1982. A study of creativity in relation to intelligence, manifest anxiety and level of aspiration of high school girls. *Doctoral Thesis*, Agra University.

Raina, M.K. 1968. A study of some correlates of creativity in Indian students. *Doctoral Thesis,* University of Rajastan.

——— 1969. A study of sex differences in creativity in India. *Journal of Creative Behaviour,* 3, 111-114.

———- 1970. A study of creativity in teachers. *Psychological Studies,* 15, 1 & 2, 28-33.

——— 1971. Verbal and non-verbal creative thinking ability: A study in sex differences. *Journal of Education and Psychology,* 29, 3, 175-179.

Rogers, 1962. Client centered therapy its current practice, implications and therapy, Boston, Houghton Mifflin.

Rogers, C.R. 1962. Toward a theory of creativity (In) Parnes, S.J. and Harding, H.F. (Eds.). *A source book for creative thinking* 63-2. Scribner, New York.

——— 1969. Toward a theory of creativity (In) Anderson, H.D. (Ed.,) *Creativity and its Cultivation,* Harper and Row, New York, 70.

Razik, T.M.A. An investigation of creative thinking among college students. *Dissertation Abstracts,* 24, 7, 2775.

Ruth, Jen-Evik and Birren James, E. 1985. Creativity in adult hood and oldage, relations to intelligence, sex and mode of testing. *International Journal of Behavioural Development,* 8, 1, 99-107

Rawat, M.S. and Garg, M.K. 1977. A study of creativity and level of aspiration of high school students. *Indian Psychological Review,* 14, 2, 51-53.

Rasool, G. 1977. A study of divergent thinking of school going children. *Creativity News Letter,* 6, 2, 23-26.

Ramachandra, Mohanty and Katiyar, P.C. 1986. A study of creativity in relation to intelligence, academic achievement and problem solving ability of students. *M.Phil Abstract,* Devi Ahalya Viswavidyalayam, Indore.

Ray Chaudhuri, 1965. Personality correlates of creativity. Samiskha, 19, 3, 107-134.

Rehman, A. and Jussain, M.G. 1973. Creativity and social desirability. *The Educational Trends,* 8, 1-4, 163-165.

Raja Sekhar Reddy, T. 1997. Creativity of student teachers of DIETS in relaion to certain variables. *Unpublished M.Phil, Dissertation,* Maduraikamaraj University, Madurai.

Rawat, M.S. and Agarwal, S. 1977. A study of creative thinking with reference to intelligence, age, sex, communities and income group. *Indian Psychological Review,*14, 2, 36-40.

Syama Thirumurthy, 1987. Creative thinking ability as a function of sex, intelligence and study habits. *Journal of Education and Psychology*, 45, 1, 51, 56.

Sansanwal, D.N. and Jarial, Gurpal Singh, 1979. Personality differences among high and low creative teacher trainees. *Journal of the Institute of Educational Research*. 3, 3, 24-26.

——1980 Creativity and age. *Creativity News Letter* (In Press).

—— 1981 (In) Passi B.K. 1982. Creativity in Education, *National Psychological Corporation*, Agra.

Shukla, Prakash Chandra, 1982. A study of creativity in relation to sex, locality and school subjects. *Indian Educational Review*,17, 2, 128-132.

Simpson, R.M. 1922. Creative Imagination. *American Journal of Psychology*, 33, 234-243.

Singer, J.L. 1961. Imagination and waiting ability in young children. *Journal of Personality*, 29, 396-413.

Sharma, K.N. 1974. Creativity as a function of intelligence Fine arts intersts and culture. *Indian Journal of Psychology*, 49, 4, 313-319.

Sharma, A.K. and Jarial, G.S., Katiyar, 1980. Factorial study of the effect of SES, grade levels and their interaction upon creativity and its components. *Trends in Education*, 7, 1 and 2, 37-42.

Saxena, Saroja. 1981. A study of need achievement in relation to creativity, values, leels of aspiration and anxiety. *Doctoral Thesis*, Agra University.

Sen Gupta, M. 1982. Purdue Creativity Test. Psychometric Properties on an Indian Sample. *Psychological Studies*. 27, 1, 23-28.

Seetharam, R. and Vedanayagam, E.G. 1979. Creativity and Socio-economic status. *Journal of the Institute of Educational Research*, 3, 4, 35-37.

Sharma, A.K. 1980. Creativity and its components as affected by Socio-economic status and personality. *Experiments in Education*, 8, 7, 129-133.

Straus, J.H. and Straus. M.A. 1968. Family roles and sex differences in creativity in children in Bombay and Minneapolis. *Journal of Marriage and Family*. 30, 1, 46-53.

Singh, D. 1978. A study of the personality correlates of creativity children (15+) studying science subjects. *Doctoral Thesis*, Bhopal University.

——1979. Personality correlates of creative children studying in science subjects. *Doctoral Thesis*, Bhopal University.

Sivarathnam Reddy, 1994. A study of creativity of students at +2 level in relation to some variables. *Ph.D.Thesis*, S.V.University, Tirupati.

Sudhakar Reddy, P.1990. An investigation into the creativity of adolescent boys and girls. *Ph.D., Thesis*, S.V.University, Tirupati.

Stein, M.I. 1960. Transactional approach to creativity (In) Taylor, C-W and Frank Barron (Eds) Scientific Creativity: Its recognition and development, John Willey and Sons, Inc., New York.

——— and Heinze, S.J. 1960. Creativity and the individual. Free Press of Glencoe, Inc., Glencoe.

The Encyclopedia of Britannica (1951) *Dictionary of Education*, McGraw Hill Company, New York.

The Indian Education Commission (1982) Ministry of Education, Government of India, New Delhi.

The National Policy on Education (1986). In the textbook *"Teaching of Science Today and Tomorrow'* by Siddique and Siddique.

1960 The creative individual. A New Protrait in Giftedness. *Educational Leadership*, 18, 1, 7-12.

Taylor, C.W. 1964. Creativity: *Progress and Potential*, McGraw Hill, New York.

Terman, L.M. (1925) Genetic Studies of Genious. *Vol. I Mental & Physical Traits of a Thousand Gifted Children*. Stanford University Press, Stonford, California.

——— 1937, *Measuring Intelligence*, Houghton. Mifflin. Borton.

Thamma Pratap, V. 1976. A Comparative study of creativity of Indian Students (Baroda) and Thai students (Nakornsawan) of Grade IX. *Unpublished M.Ed., Dissertation*, M.S.University, Baroda.

Thorndike, R.L. 1963. Some methodological issues in study of creativity (IN) Gardner, E.F. (Ed) *Proceedings of 1962 Invitational Conference on Testing Problems*. Princeton: Educational Testing Service.

Trow Bridge. N. 1966. Research on creativity (In) Patel. A.S. and Shah G.B. (Eds.) *Education of Backward and the Gifted Children*. Centre for Advanced study in Education. Baroda.

Trivedi, R.C. 1969. To establish the reliability and validity of the tests of creativity. *Unpublished M.Ed., Dissertation*, Punjab University.

Tonbee, A. 1964. Is America neglecting her creative minority (In) Taylor, C.W.(Ed). *Widening Horizons in Creativity*. John Willey and Sons Inc., New York.

Torrance, E.P. 1961. Status of knowledge concerning education and creative scientific talent. *Working paper for a project on the status of knowledge about creative scientific talent,* directed by Taylor, C.W.University of Utah, with support by the National Science Foundations.

——1962, *Guiding Creative Talent,* Prentice Hall (Indian Reprint, 1969)

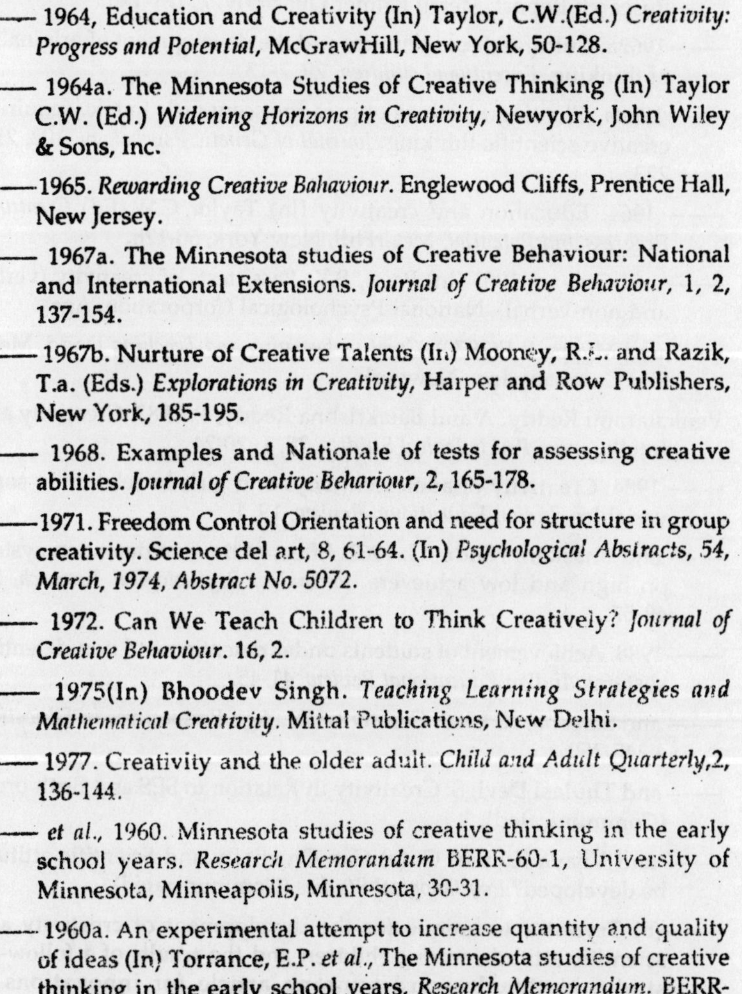

——1963, *Education and the Creative Potential.* Minneapolis, University of Minnesota Press, Minnesota.

—— 1964, Education and Creativity (In) Taylor, C.W.(Ed.) *Creativity: Progress and Potential,* McGrawHill, New York, 50-128.

—— 1964a. The Minnesota Studies of Creative Thinking (In) Taylor C.W. (Ed.) *Widening Horizons in Creativity,* Newyork, John Wiley & Sons, Inc.

——1965. *Rewarding Creative Bahaviour.* Englewood Cliffs, Prentice Hall, New Jersey.

—— 1967a. The Minnesota studies of Creative Behaviour: National and International Extensions. *Journal of Creative Behaviour,* 1, 2, 137-154.

——1967b. Nurture of Creative Talents (In) Mooney, R.L. and Razik, T.a. (Eds.) *Explorations in Creativity,* Harper and Row Publishers, New York, 185-195.

—— 1968. Examples and Nationale of tests for assessing creative abilities. *Journal of Creative Behariour,* 2, 165-178.

——1971. Freedom Control Orientation and need for structure in group creativity. Science del art, 8, 61-64. (In) *Psychological Abstracts,* 54, *March, 1974, Abstract No. 5072.*

—— 1972. Can We Teach Children to Think Creatively? *Journal of Creative Behaviour.* 16, 2.

—— 1975(In) Bhoodev Singh. *Teaching Learning Strategies and Mathematical Creativity.* Mittal Publications, New Delhi.

——1977. Creativity and the older adult. *Child and Adult Quarterly,*2, 136-144.

—— *et al.,* 1960. Minnesota studies of creative thinking in the early school years. *Research Memorandum* BERR-60-1, University of Minnesota, Minneapolis, Minnesota, 30-31.

——1960a. An experimental attempt to increase quantity and quality of ideas (In) Torrance, E.P. *et al.,* The Minnesota studies of creative thinking in the early school years, *Research Memorandum.* BERR-60-1, University of Minnesota, Minneapolis, Minnesota, 30-31.

——1960b. Exploration in creative thinking. *Education,* 18, 216-220.

Tarrance E.P. and his associates 1960c. Exploration in creative thinking in the early school years. XI changing reactions of girls in grades four through six to tasks requiring creative scientific thinking. *Research Memorandum* No.60-12 University of Minnesota, Bureall of Educational Research, Minneapolis, Minnesota.

—— 1961. Factors affecting creative thinking in children. An interim Research Report. Merril Palmer Quarterly, 7, 171-180.

——1962a. Cultural discontinuities and the development of originality of thinking. *Exceptional children*, 29, 2-13.

—— 1963a. Chaning reactions of preadolescent girls to take requiring creative scientific thinking. *Journal of Genetic Psychology*, 102, 217-223.

—— 1964. Education and creativity (In) Taylor C.W.(Ed) *Creativity Progress and Potential*, McGrHill, New York, 50-128.

—— and Gowan, 1963 (In) Passi, B.K. Passi tests of creativity (verbal and non-verbal), National Psychological Corporation, Agra.

——and Myers, R.E(1970). *Creative Learning and Teaching* Dodd, Mead and Company Inc., Newyork.

Venkatarami Reddy. A and Balakrishna Reddy, P. 1983. Creativity and Intelligence. *Psychological Studies*. 28, 1, 20-24.

—— 1984. Creativity of adolescent boys and girls in relation to some variables, *Indian Educational Review*, 19, 1.

——and Bhaskara Naidu, G. 1962. Effect of the non detention system on high and low achievers. *Journal of Psychological Research*, 26, 49-57.

——1988. Achievement of students under detention and non-detention systems. *Indian Educational Review*, 41-45.

——and Saleena, K. 1988. Creativity Vs. Age *Perspectives in Education*, 4,245-250.

——and Thulasi Devi, S. Creativity in Relation to SES and Birth order (Communicated).

—— and Vijaya Kumari G. (a) Can Creativity and Scientific attitude be developed? *Psychological Studies* (Communicated).

——(b) Tryout a technique for the development of creativity and scientific attitude among children and the results of a follow-up study. National award winning article for innovations in Education, presented and discussed at the Education Conference held from 29-3-1989 to 2-4-1989 at the National Council for Educational Research and Training Campus, Ajmer.

Vohra, I.N. 1975. A study of non-verbal creativity in relation to socio-economic status, age, medium of instruction and personality characteristics amongst the pupils of English and Gujarati medium of "Bazm-E-Hidayat" Primary School from Baroda city. *Unpublished M.Ed Dissertation,* M.S. University.

Vinake, 1952. *The Psychology of Thinking* McGrawHill New York.

Vernon, P.E. 1964. Creativity and Intelligence Educational Research 6, 163-176.

Verma, L.K. 1980. A study of locus of control of high and low creative school students at different levels of socio-economic status. *Journal of Education and Psychology,* 38, 2, 99-104.

Verma, R.S. 1973. A factor analytic study of divergent thinking in relation to certain personality dimensions of higher secondary school adolescents. *Doctoral Thesis* Aligarh Muslim University.

Zargar, A.H. and Neelam Dhar. 1988. Creativity and Socio-economic Status: A study. *The Education Review,* XCIV, 29-31.

Zargar, A.H. 1983. Creativity and Neuroticism: A correlational analysis, *The Educational Review,* 89, 91-93.

Yomamoto, K. 1960. The role of creative thinking and intelligence in high school achievement. *Research Memorandum,* BER-60-10. Bureau of Educational Research, College of Education, University of Minnesota, 1-245.

——1961. Creativity and Intellect: Review of Current Research and Protection. *Paper presented at Minnesota Psychological Association,* Minneapolis.

——1964a. Experimental scoring manuals for Minnesota tests of creative thinking and writing. *Kent Bureau of Educational Research,* Kent State, University, Kent, Ohio.

——1964b. Creative thinking. Some thoughts on research. *Exceptional children,* 403-410.

——1965. Effects of restriction of range and test unreliability on correlation between measures of intelligence and creative thinking. *British Journal of Educational Psychology,* 35, 300-305.

Wilson, R.G., and Lewis, D.J. 1954—A factor analytical study of creative thinking abilities. *Psychometrics,* 19, 297-311.

Wilson, R.C., Guilford, J.P. and Christianson, P.R. 1974. (In) Dutt, N.K. Psychological Foundation of Education, Deoba House, Delhi, 208.

Wodtke, K.H. 1964. Some data on the reliability and validity of creativity tests at the elementary school level. Educational and Psychological Measurement, 24, 2, 339-408.

Wallach, M. and Kogan, N. 1965. Modes of Thinking in young children, Hott, Rinehart and Winston Inc., New York.

Wallas, G. 1926. The Art of thought. Harcourt brace & world, Inc., New York.

Watson, G. 1957. Some personality difference in children related strict or permissive parental discipline. *Journal of Psychology,* 44, 227-49.

Walker, P.C. 1969. A study of creativity among Mexican school children. *Doctoral Dissertation,* University of Georgia.

Index

I

J

K

L

M